"COME BE MY FOLLOWER"

THIS BOOK IS THE PROPERTY OF

_____

Publishers
WATCHTOWER BIBLE AND TRACT SOCIETY OF NEW YORK, INC.
Brooklyn, New York, U.S.A.
2007 Printing

This publication is provided as part of a worldwide
Bible educational work supported by voluntary donations.

Unless otherwise indicated, Scripture quotations
are from the modern-language
New World Translation of the Holy Scriptures—With References

Photo Credits:
Page 39: Cover of book: J. Hester and P. Scowen (AZ State Univ.), NASA;
page 87: © Tim Lynch/Index Stock Imagery

"Come Be My Follower"
English (*cf*-E)

Made in the United States of America

Dear Reader:

"Come be my follower." (Mark 10:21) With those words, Jesus Christ, in effect, beckons us to follow him. Are you responding to his call? Doing so will have a profound influence on your life. Why?

Jehovah sent his only-begotten Son to the earth to give his life as a ransom. (John 3:16) In addition to dying for us, that Son showed us how to live. With each step he took, he kept his integrity and brought joy to his Father's heart. Jesus also showed us how to be like his Father. The ways and the will of the Father found perfect expression in the words and deeds of the Son.—John 14:9.

Jesus is "a model," the Bible says, "for [us] to follow his steps closely." (1 Peter 2:21) If we want to draw closer to Jehovah, if we want to have a truly meaningful life now, and if we want to remain on the road to everlasting life, we must follow closely in the footsteps of Christ.

To begin this journey, we need to become familiar with Jesus' life on earth. So the portrait of Jesus preserved in the Bible merits our careful study. Reflecting on the things Jesus said and did and considering how we can imitate him in word and deed will help us to see more clearly how to follow him.

May this publication help you to grow in your love for Jesus and for Jehovah. And may that love move you to follow closely in Jesus' footsteps so that you may bring joy to Jehovah's heart now and forever.

The Publishers

Contents

Chapter	Page
1 "Be My Follower"—What Did Jesus Mean?	5
2 "The Way and the Truth and the Life"	15

SECTION 1   "Come and See" the Christ

3 "I Am . . . Lowly in Heart"	25
4 "Look! The Lion That Is of the Tribe of Judah"	35
5 "All the Treasures of Wisdom"	46
6 "He Learned Obedience"	56
7 "Consider Closely the One Who Has Endured"	66

SECTION 2   "Teaching . . . and Preaching the Good News"

8 "For This I Was Sent Forth"	77
9 "Go . . . and Make Disciples"	87
10 "It Is Written"	98
11 "Never Has Another Man Spoken Like This"	108
12 "Without an Illustration He Would Not Speak to Them"	118

SECTION 3   "The Love the Christ Has Compels Us"

13 "I Love the Father"	129
14 "Great Crowds Approached Him"	139
15 "Moved With Pity"	150
16 "Jesus . . . Loved Them to the End"	161
17 "No One Has Love Greater Than This"	172
18 "Continue Following Me"	182

CHAPTER 1

"Be My Follower"
—What Did Jesus Mean?

WHAT is the best invitation you have ever received? You might think of a time when you were invited to attend a special occasion, perhaps the wedding of two people very dear to you. Or you might recall the day you were invited to take on an important job. If such invitations have come your way, you were no doubt thrilled, even honored, to get them. The truth is, though, that you have received a far better invitation. Each one of us has. And the way we choose to respond to that invitation affects us profoundly. It is the most important choice we will make in life.

2 What is that invitation? It comes from Jesus Christ, the only-begotten Son of Almighty God, Jehovah, and it is recorded in the Bible. At Mark 10:21, we read Jesus' words: "Come be my follower." That is, in effect, Jesus' invitation to each one of us. We do well to ask ourselves, 'How will I respond?' The answer might appear to be obvious. Who would refuse such a splendid invitation? Surprisingly, most people do refuse. Why?

3 Consider as an example a man who received that invitation in person some 2,000 years ago. He was a highly respected man. He had at least three things that humans

1, 2. What is the best invitation a human could receive, and what question might we ask ourselves?
3, 4. (a) What might be considered enviable about the man who approached Jesus to inquire about everlasting life? (b) What good qualities might Jesus have seen in the wealthy young ruler?

"What must I do to inherit everlasting life?"   5

tend to consider desirable, even enviable—youth, wealth, and power. The Bible record describes him as a "young man," as "very rich," and as a "ruler." (Matthew 19:20; Luke 18:18, 23) However, there was something more important about this young man. He had heard of the Great Teacher, Jesus, and he liked what he had heard.

[4] Most rulers in those days failed to give Jesus the respect he deserved. (John 7:48; 12:42) But this ruler acted differently. The Bible tells us: "As [Jesus] was going out on his way, a certain man ran up and fell upon his knees before him and put the question to him: 'Good Teacher, what must I do to inherit everlasting life?'" (Mark 10:17) Notice how eager this man was to speak with Jesus, running up to him out in the open, just as any of the poor and lowly people might have done. Further, he knelt respectfully before Christ. So he had a measure of humility and an awareness of his spiritual need. Jesus valued such good qualities. (Matthew 5:3; 18:4) Little wonder, then, that "Jesus looked upon him and felt love for him." (Mark 10:21) How did Jesus answer the young man's question?

The Invitation of a Lifetime

[5] Jesus showed that his Father had already supplied information on the vital question about gaining everlasting life. He pointed to the Scriptures, and the young man affirmed that he was faithfully obeying the Mosaic Law. Jesus, however, with his extraordinary insight, saw what was below the surface. (John 2:25) He perceived a spiritual problem in this ruler—a serious one. Hence, Jesus said: "One thing is missing about you." What was that

---

5. How did Jesus respond to the wealthy young man, and how do we know that poverty was not the "one thing" missing about him? (See also footnote.)

"one thing"? Jesus said: "Go, sell what things you have and give to the poor." (Mark 10:21) Did Jesus mean that a person must be penniless in order to serve God? No.* Christ was revealing something of great importance.

6 To lay bare what was missing, Jesus offered the man a wonderful opportunity: "Come be my follower." Just imagine—the Son of the Most High God invited that man, face-to-face, to follow him! Jesus also promised him a reward beyond imagination. He said: "You will have treasure in heaven." Did the wealthy young ruler seize this opportunity, this glorious invitation? The account reads: "He grew sad at the saying and went off grieved, for he was holding many possessions." (Mark 10: 21, 22) So Jesus' unexpected words revealed a problem in the heart of this man. He was too deeply attached to his possessions and, no doubt, to the power and prestige that came with them. Sadly, his love for such things far outweighed any love he had for Christ. The "one thing" missing, then, was wholehearted, self-sacrificing love for Jesus and Jehovah. Because the young man lacked such love, he turned down the invitation of a lifetime! How, though, are you involved?

7 Jesus' invitation was not limited to that man; nor was it restricted to just a few people. Jesus said: "If anyone

_____

* Jesus did not ask everyone who followed him to give up all possessions. And although he did comment on how difficult it is for a rich person to enter the Kingdom of God, he added: "All things are possible with God." (Mark 10:23, 27) In fact, a few wealthy people did become Christ's followers. They received specific counsel in the Christian congregation, but they were not asked to donate all their wealth to the poor.—1 Timothy 6:17.

_____

6. What invitation did Jesus offer, and what did the wealthy young ruler's response reveal about his heart?
7. Why may we be sure that Jesus' invitation includes us today?

wants to come after me, let him . . . follow me continually." (Luke 9:23) Notice that <u>"anyone" can be Christ's follower if he truly "wants to."</u> God draws such honeshleart-
ed ones to his Son. (John 6:44) Not just the rich, not just
the poor, not just those of a certain race or nation, and
not just those living during that time period but <u>*all* are</u>
<u>given an opportunity to accept Jesus' invitation.</u> So Jesus'
words "Come be my follower" really do apply to you.
Why should you want to follow Christ? And just what is
involved?

Why Be a Follower of Christ?

8 There is a truth that we should acknowledge: We have
a profound need for <u>good leadership</u>. Not all humans ad-
mit to having that need, but it is there nonetheless. Jehovah's prophet Jeremiah was inspired to record this eternal truth: "I well know, O Jehovah, that to earthling man
his way does not belong. It does not belong to man who
is walking even to direct his step." (Jeremiah 10:23) <u>Hu-</u>
<u>mans have neither the ability nor the right</u> to govern
<u>themselves.</u> Indeed, human history is largely a record of
bad leadership. (Ecclesiastes 8:9) In Jesus' day, the leaders
oppressed, abused, and misled the people. Jesus astutely
observed that the common people were "as sheep without a shepherd." (Mark 6:34) The same is true of mankind today. As a group and as individuals, <u>we need leader-</u>
<u>ship we can trust and respect.</u> Does Jesus meet that need?
Consider several reasons why the answer is yes.

9 First, *Jesus was chosen by Jehovah God.* Most human
leaders are chosen by their fellow imperfect humans,
who are often deceived and who tend to misjudge. Jesus

---

8. What need do all humans have, and why?
9. What sets Jesus apart from all other leaders?

is a different kind of leader. His very title tells us that. The word "Christ," like the word "Messiah," means "Anointed One." Yes, Jesus was anointed, or specially appointed to his sacred office, by none other than the Sovereign Lord of the universe. Jehovah God said of his Son: "Look! My servant whom I chose, my beloved, whom my soul approved! I will put my spirit upon him." (Matthew 12: 18) No one knows better than our Creator what kind of leader we need. Jehovah's wisdom is infinite, so we have ample reason to trust his selection.—Proverbs 3:5, 6.

¹⁰ Second, *Jesus set a perfect and an inspiring example for us.* The best kind of leader has qualities that his subjects can admire and imitate. He leads by example, inspiring others to become better than they were. What qualities would you respect the most in a leader? Courage? Wisdom? Compassion? What about perseverance in the face of hardship? As you study the record of Jesus' life course on earth, you will find that he possessed those qualities —and more. The perfect reflection of his heavenly Father, Jesus possessed every divine quality in full measure. He was all that a perfect human could be. So in everything that he did, in every word that he uttered, in every inner feeling that he revealed, we find something worth imitating. The Bible says that he provided "a model for you to follow his steps closely."—1 Peter 2:21.

¹¹ Third, *Christ fully lived up to his claim: "I am the fine shepherd."* (John 10:14) To people in Bible times, that figure of speech struck a familiar chord. Shepherds worked hard to take care of the sheep in their charge. A "fine shepherd" would put the safety and well-being of the flock ahead of his own. Jesus' ancestor David, for

10. Why is Jesus' example the best one for humans to follow?
11. How did Jesus prove to be "the fine shepherd"?

example, was a shepherd as a youth, and on more than one occasion, he risked his life to fight off an attack on his sheep by a vicious wild animal. (1 Samuel 17:34-36) Jesus went even further in behalf of his human followers. He laid down his life for them. (John 10:15) How many leaders have such a self-sacrificing spirit?

[12] Jesus was "the fine shepherd" in another sense. He said: "I know my sheep and my sheep know me." (John 10:14) Think of the word picture that Jesus was painting. To a casual observer, a flock of sheep might seem just a mass of woolly creatures. The shepherd, however, knows each sheep individually. He knows which ewes will soon need his aid when they give birth, which lambs still need to be carried because they are too tiny and weak to walk far on their own, and which sheep have recently been ill or injured. The sheep know their shepherd as well. They recognize his voice, never mistaking it for that of any other shepherd. When there is a tone of alarm or urgency in his call, they respond quickly. Where he leads, they follow. And he knows just where to lead them. He knows where the grass is lush and green, where the streams are fresh and clear, where the pastures are safe. As he watches over them, the sheep sense that they are secure. —Psalm 23.

[13] Do you not long for leadership like that? The Fine Shepherd has an incomparable record in treating his followers just that way. He promises to guide you to a happy and fulfilling life now and on into an eternal future! (John 10:10, 11; Revelation 7:16, 17) We need to know, then, just what is involved in following Christ.

12, 13. (a) In what sense does a shepherd know his sheep, and in what way do they know him? (b) Why do you want to be under the leadership of the Fine Shepherd?

What It Means to Be a Follower of Christ

¹⁴ Hundreds of millions of people today likely feel that they have accepted Christ's invitation. After all, they choose to call themselves Christians. Perhaps they belong to the church in which their parents had them christened. Or they may claim to have an emotional attachment to Jesus and accept him as their personal Savior. But does that make them followers of Christ? Is that what Jesus had in mind when he invited us to become his followers? There is much more to it.

¹⁵ Consider the world of Christendom—those nations whose citizens for the most part claim to be followers of Christ. Does Christendom reflect the teachings of Jesus Christ? Or do we see in those lands hatred, oppression, crime, and injustice much like that found throughout the rest of the world? The respected Hindu leader Mohandas Gandhi once said: "I know of no one who has done more for humanity than Jesus. In fact, there is nothing wrong with Christianity." He added: "The trouble is with you Christians. You do not begin to live up to your own teachings."

¹⁶ Jesus said that his true followers would be known not just for their words or for the label they apply to themselves but primarily for their actions. For example, he said: "Not everyone saying to me, 'Lord, Lord,' will enter into the kingdom of the heavens, but the one doing the will of my Father who is in the heavens will." (Matthew 7:21) Why do so many who claim Jesus as their Lord fail to do his Father's will? Remember the wealthy young

14, 15. In order to be a follower of Christ, why is it not enough to claim to be a Christian or to form an emotional attachment to Jesus?
16, 17. What is often missing among professed Christians, and what distinguishes genuine followers of Christ?

ruler. All too often, "one thing is missing" among professed Christians—whole-souled love for Jesus and for the One who sent him forth.

17 How can that be? Do not millions who call themselves Christians also claim to love Christ? No doubt. But love for Jesus and for Jehovah involves far more than words. Jesus said: "If anyone loves me, he will observe my word." (John 14:23) And again speaking as a shepherd, he said: "My sheep listen to my voice, and I know them, and they follow me." (John 10:27) Yes, the true test of our love for Christ is not merely in our words or in our feelings but mainly in our actions.

18 Our actions, however, do not simply spring from nowhere. They reflect the person we are deep inside. It is here that our work must begin. Jesus said: "This means everlasting life, their taking in knowledge of you, the only true God, and of the one whom you sent forth, Jesus Christ." (John 17:3) If we take in and meditate on accurate knowledge about Jesus, our heart will be affected. We will come to love him more and more, building in ourselves an ever greater desire to follow him day by day.

19 Herein lies the purpose of this book. Its aim is, not to give a complete summary of the life and ministry of Jesus, but to help us see more clearly how to follow him.* It is designed to help us look into the mirror of Scripture and ask ourselves, 'Am I truly following Jesus?' (James 1:23-25) Perhaps you have long considered yourself to

---

* For a full, chronological summary of the events of Jesus' life and ministry, see *The Greatest Man Who Ever Lived*, published by Jehovah's Witnesses.

18, 19. (a) How should learning about Jesus affect us? (b) What is the purpose of this book, and how will it benefit those who have long considered themselves to be followers of Christ?

Invitations From God's Only-Begotten Son

Imagine that Jesus is directing the following invitations to you personally. How would you respond, and why?

"Be my follower."—Matthew 9:9; Luke 9:59; John 1:43.

"If anyone wants to come after me, let him disown himself and pick up his torture stake and continually follow me."—Matthew 16:24.

"Come to me, all you who are toiling and loaded down, and I will refresh you. Take my yoke upon you and learn from me."—Matthew 11:28, 29.

"If anyone is thirsty, let him come to me and drink."—John 7:37.

---

be a sheep guided by the Fine Shepherd. Would you not agree, though, that we can always find ways to improve? The Bible urges us: "Keep testing whether you are in the faith, keep proving what you yourselves are." (2 Corinthians 13:5) It is worth our every effort to make sure that we are indeed being guided by our loving Fine Shepherd, Jesus, whom Jehovah himself has appointed to lead us.

[20] May your study of this book help you to strengthen your love for Jesus and for Jehovah. As such love guides you in life, you will find the greatest measure of peace and contentment possible in this old world, and you will live to praise Jehovah forever for providing us with the Fine Shepherd. Of course, our study of Christ must be based on the right foundation. It is fitting, then, that in Chapter 2 we will examine Jesus' role in Jehovah's universal purpose.

---

20. What will we consider in the following chapter?

"The Way and the Truth and the Life"

HAVE you ever been lost? You may recall an occasion when you were traveling to visit a friend or a relative and could not find the way. As you proceeded along an unfamiliar road, did you stop and ask someone for directions? Imagine how you would feel if, instead of just telling you which way to go, a benevolent individual said: "Just follow me. I will lead you there." How relieved you would be!

² In a sense, Jesus Christ does something like that for us. On our own, approach to God would be impossible. Because of inherited sin and imperfection, the world of mankind is lost, "alienated from the life that belongs to God." (Ephesians 4:17, 18) We need help to find our way. Jesus, our benevolent Exemplar, does not just offer advice and directions; he does more. As we saw in Chapter 1, Jesus invites us, saying: "Come be my follower." (Mark 10:21) However, he also gives us compelling reason to accept that invitation. On one occasion, Jesus said: "I am the way and the truth and the life. No one comes to the Father except through me." (John 14:6) Let us discuss some reasons why approach to the Father is possible only through the Son. Then with those reasons in mind, we will consider how Jesus is, indeed, "the way and the truth and the life."

1, 2. Why would approach to Jehovah be impossible on our own, and what has Jesus Christ done for us in this regard?

A Vital Place in Jehovah's Purpose

³ First and foremost, approach to God is through Jesus because Jehovah has seen fit to give his Son the most important role.* The Father has made him the central, or key, figure in the outworking of all of His purposes. (2 Corinthians 1:20; Colossians 1:18-20) To understand the vital role of the Son, we need to consider what happened in the garden of Eden, where the first human couple joined Satan in rebelling against Jehovah.—Genesis 2: 16, 17; 3:1-6.

⁴ The rebellion in Eden raised an issue of universal importance: Does Jehovah God properly exercise his rulership over his creatures? To settle this vital issue, Jehovah determined that a perfect spirit son would have to go to earth. The mission that this son would carry out could not have been weightier—giving his life to vindicate Jehovah's sovereignty and to serve as a ransom to save humankind. By remaining faithful to death, the son chosen would make it possible to solve all the problems raised by Satan's rebellion. (Hebrews 2:14, 15; 1 John 3:8) But Jehovah had millions upon millions of perfect spirit sons. (Daniel 7:9, 10) Which one did he select to carry out this most important assignment? Jehovah chose his "only-begotten Son," the one who later came to be known as Jesus Christ.—John 3:16.

⁵ Should we be surprised at Jehovah's choice? By no means! The Father had the utmost confidence in his only-

---

* So important is the role of the Son that the Bible gives him a number of prophetic names and titles.—See the box on page 23.

3. Why is approach to God through Jesus?
4. The rebellion in Eden raised what issue, and what did Jehovah determine to do in order to settle the issue?
5, 6. How did Jehovah demonstrate that he had confidence in his Son, and upon what was this confidence based?

begotten Son. Centuries in advance of the arrival of his Son on earth, Jehovah foretold that this Son would remain loyal despite undergoing all manner of suffering. (Isaiah 53:3-7, 10-12; Acts 8:32-35) Consider the implications of that. The Son, like all other intelligent creatures, was a free moral agent, able to choose his own course. Yet, Jehovah had such confidence that he foretold the faithfulness of his Son. Upon what was this confidence based? In a word, knowledge. Jehovah knows his Son intimately and knows how much his Son wants to please Him. (John 8:29; 14:31) The Son loves his Father, and in turn, Jehovah loves His Son. (John 3:35) The love that Father and Son have for each other forges between them a bond of unity and trust that is unbreakable.—Colossians 3:14.

⁶ In view of the important role of the Son, the confidence that the Father has in him, and the love that binds the Father and the Son together, is it any wonder that approach to God is possible only through Jesus? Yet, there is another reason why the Son alone can lead us to the Father.

Only the Son Fully Knows the Father

⁷ There are requirements to be met if we are to gain access to Jehovah. (Psalm 15:1-5) Who knows better than the Son what it takes to meet God's standards and to have His approval? Jesus said: "All things have been delivered to me by my Father, and no one fully knows the Son but the Father, neither does anyone fully know the Father but the Son and anyone to whom the Son is willing to reveal him." (Matthew 11:27) Let us see why Jesus could say, correctly and without exaggerating, that no one fully knows the Father "but the Son."

7, 8. Why could Jesus correctly say that no one fully knows the Father "but the Son"?

⁸ As "the firstborn of all creation," the Son has unique intimacy with Jehovah. (Colossians 1:15) Imagine the closeness of the Father-Son relationship that developed during the untold ages when it was just the two of them—from the dawn of creation until other spirit creatures were brought into existence. (John 1:3; Colossians 1:16, 17) Just think about the precious opportunity the Son had alongside his Father, absorbing the Father's thoughts on matters and learning His will, standards, and ways. Truly, it is by no means an overstatement to say that Jesus knows his Father better than anyone else does. This closeness surely enabled Jesus to reveal his Father in ways that no one else could.

⁹ The teachings of Jesus reflected his keen awareness of how Jehovah thinks and feels and of what He requires of His worshippers.* Jesus revealed his Father in yet another profound way. Jesus said: "He that has seen me has seen the Father also." (John 14:9) Jesus perfectly imitated his Father in everything he said and did. So when we read in the Bible about Jesus—the powerful and winsome words that he used in his teaching, the compassion that moved him to heal others, and the empathy that caused him to give way to tears—we might well picture Jehovah saying and doing those very things. (Matthew 7:28, 29; Mark 1:40-42; John 11:32-36) The ways and will of the Father are perfectly revealed in the words and actions of the Son. (John 5:19; 8:28; 12:49, 50) Thus, to have Jehovah's approval, we need to heed the teachings of Jesus and follow his example.—John 14:23.

---

* See, for example, Jesus' words recorded at Matthew 10:29-31; 18:12-14, 21-35; 22:36-40.

9, 10. (a) In what ways did Jesus reveal his Father? (b) To have Jehovah's approval, what must we do?

¹⁰ Since Jesus knows Jehovah intimately and imitates him perfectly, it is not surprising that Jehovah has determined that the Son is the means for approaching the Father. With this foundation for understanding why we can come to Jehovah only through Jesus, let us now discuss the meaning of Jesus' words: "I am the way and the truth and the life. No one comes to the Father except through me."—John 14:6.

"I Am the Way"

¹¹ We have already learned that there is no approach to God without going through Jesus. Consider, more specifically, what this means for us. Jesus is "the way" in that only through him can we enter into an approved relationship with God. Why is that so? By proving faithful to death, Jesus gave his life as a ransom sacrifice. (Matthew 20:28) Without this ransom provision, it would be impossible for us to have access to God. Sin creates a barrier between humans and God, for Jehovah is holy and therefore can never approve of sin. (Isaiah 6:3; 59:2) But the sacrifice of Jesus removed the barrier; it provided the necessary covering, or atonement, for sin. (Hebrews 10:12; 1 John 1:7) If we accept God's provision through Christ and put faith in it, we can enter into Jehovah's favor. There is simply no other way for us to become "reconciled to God."*—Romans 5:6-11.

¹² Jesus is "the way" when it comes to prayer. Only

---

* At John 14:6, the use of the personal pronoun "I" along with the definite article, "the," stresses that Jesus' position is unique, that he is the way, the only one through whom we can approach the Father.

---

11. (a) Why can we enter into an approved relationship with God only through Jesus? (b) How do the words recorded at John 14:6 stress the uniqueness of Jesus' position? (See footnote.)
12. Jesus is "the way" in what senses?

through Jesus can we go to Jehovah in prayer with the
assurance that our heartfelt petitions will be favorably
heard. (1 John 5:13, 14) Jesus himself said: "If you ask the
Father for anything he will give it to you in my name. . . .
Ask and you will receive, that your joy may be made full."
(John 16:23, 24) Appropriately, in the name of Jesus, we
can approach Jehovah in prayer and call Him "our Father." (Matthew 6:9) Jesus is "the way" in yet another
sense—by his example. As noted earlier, Jesus perfectly
imitated his Father. Jesus' example thus shows us how to
live so as to please Jehovah. To approach Jehovah, then,
we must walk in the footsteps of Jesus.—1 Peter 2:21.

"I Am . . . the Truth"

[13] Jesus always spoke the truth about his Father's prophetic word. (John 8:40, 45, 46) No deception was ever
found in Jesus' mouth. (1 Peter 2:22) Even his opposers acknowledged that he taught "the way of God in line
with truth." (Mark 12:13, 14) However, when Jesus said
"I am . . . the truth," he was not simply referring to the
fact that he made truth known in his speaking, preaching, and teaching. More—much more—than talking was
involved.

[14] Recall that centuries in advance, Jehovah had inspired Bible writers to record scores of prophecies about
the Messiah, or Christ. These prophecies foretold details
about his life, ministry, and death. In addition, the Mosaic Law contained shadows, or prophetic patterns, that
pointed to the Messiah. (Hebrews 10:1) Would Jesus
prove faithful to death, thereby fulfilling all the things
prophesied about him? Only then would Jehovah be vin-

13, 14. (a) How was Jesus truthful in his speech? (b) For Jesus to be
"the truth," what did he have to do, and why?

dicated as the God of true prophecy. That tremendous weight rested upon the shoulders of Jesus. By the way he lived—every word he spoke and every deed he performed—Jesus brought the prophetic patterns into the realm of actual truth. (2 Corinthians 1:20) Thus, Jesus *was* "the truth." It was as if the truth of Jehovah's prophetic word arrived in the person of Jesus.—John 1:17; Colossians 2:16, 17.

"I Am . . . the Life"

¹⁵ Jesus is "the life," for it is only through him that we can receive life—that is, "the real life." (1 Timothy 6:19) The Bible says: "He that exercises faith in the Son has everlasting life; he that disobeys the Son will not see life, but the wrath of God remains upon him." (John 3:36) What does it mean to exercise faith in the Son of God? It means that we have the conviction that we cannot gain life without him. More than that, it means that we demonstrate our faith by works, continue to learn from Jesus, and do our best to follow his teachings and example. (James 2:26) Thus, exercising faith in the Son of God leads to everlasting life—immortal spirit life in heaven for a "little flock" of spirit-anointed Christians and perfect human life in an earthly paradise for "a great crowd" of "other sheep."—Luke 12:32; 23:43; Revelation 7:9-17; John 10:16.

¹⁶ What about those who have already died? Jesus is "the life" for them as well. Shortly before he raised his friend Lazarus from the dead, Jesus told Martha, the sister of Lazarus: "I am the resurrection and the life. He that

---

15. What does it mean to exercise faith in the Son, and to what can doing so lead?
16, 17. (a) How will Jesus prove to be "the life" even for those who have died? (b) What confidence can we have?

exercises faith in me, even though he dies, will come to life." (John 11:25) Jehovah has entrusted his Son with "the keys of death and of Hades," granting him the power to resurrect. (Revelation 1:17, 18) With those keys, the glorified Jesus will unlock the gates of Hades and thus release all those being held in mankind's common grave. —John 5:28, 29.

[17] "I am the way and the truth and the life"—with this simple statement, Jesus summarized the objective of his life and ministry on earth. Those words are filled with meaning for us today. Recall that Jesus followed up this statement by saying: "No one comes to the Father except through me." (John 14:6) Jesus' words are as relevant today as they were when he uttered them. We can therefore have full confidence that if we follow Jesus, we will never become lost. He, and he alone, will show us the way "to the Father."

How Will You Respond?

[18] In view of Jesus' vital role and his intimate knowledge of the Father, we have good reason to follow the Son. As we saw in the preceding chapter, being true followers of Jesus involves actions, not just words or feelings. Following Christ involves patterning our life after his teachings and example. (John 13:15) The study aid that you are now reading can help you in this endeavor.

[19] In the chapters that follow, we will make a careful study of the life and ministry of Jesus. These chapters are divided into three sections. First, we will get an overview of his qualities and ways. Second, we will examine

18. What does being true followers of Jesus involve?
19, 20. What does this study aid contain that can help you in your endeavor to follow Christ?

Some Titles Applied to Jesus Christ

The Amen (meaning "so be it," or "surely"). He is the One in whom God's promises find sure fulfillment.—2 Corinthians 1: 19, 20.

Eternal Father. Jehovah has granted him the power and authority to give humans the prospect of eternal life in perfection on earth.—Isaiah 9:6.

High Priest. He can cleanse us from sin and liberate us from sin's death-dealing effects.—Hebrews 3:1; 9:13, 14, 25, 26.

King of kings. As a heavenly King appointed by God, Jesus is far mightier than any earthly ruler.—Revelation 17:14.

Prince of Peace. As the Ruler of God's Kingdom, Jesus will establish on earth a peace that will be global and will never end. —Isaiah 9:6.

Wonderful Counselor. Jesus' counsel is always practical and perfect. Following it leads to salvation.—Isaiah 9:6; John 6:68.

The Word. He is Jehovah's Spokesman.—John 1:1.

his zealous example in preaching and teaching. Third, we will consider how he manifested love. Starting with Chapter 3, there is a teaching box entitled "How Can You Follow Jesus?" The scriptures and questions therein are designed to help us meditate on how we can imitate Jesus in word and deed.

[20] Thanks to Jehovah God, you do not have to be lost, alienated from him because of inherited sin. At great cost to himself, Jehovah lovingly sent forth his Son to show us the way to come into an approved relationship with God. (1 John 4:9, 10) May you be moved, yes, impelled, to respond to that great love by accepting and acting upon Jesus' invitation: "Be my follower."—John 1:43.

"COME AND SEE" THE CHRIST

*Jesus lived as a man some 2,000 years ago,
yet it is still possible for us today to
"come and see" the Son of God. (John 1:46)
The Gospel accounts paint a vivid picture
of his personality, attitudes, and ways.
This section will provide an overview of
Jesus' outstanding qualities.*

"I Am . . . Lowly in Heart"

JERUSALEM is buzzing with excitement. A great man is coming! Outside the city, people gather along the road. They are eager to welcome this man, for some are saying that he is an heir of King David and the rightful Ruler of Israel. A number bring palm fronds to wave in greeting; others spread out garments and tree branches on the road to smooth the way before him. (Matthew 21:7, 8; John 12:12, 13) Many likely wonder what kind of entry he will make.

² Some may be expecting a display of magnificence. They surely know of important men who made grand entrances. For example, David's son Absalom proclaimed himself a king; he had 50 men running ahead of his chariot. (2 Samuel 15:1, 10) The Roman ruler Julius Caesar demanded even more fanfare; he once led a triumphal procession up to the Roman capitol, flanked by 40 elephants bearing lamps! Now, however, the people of Jerusalem await a far greater man. Whether the crowds fully understand that or not, this is the Messiah, the greatest man ever to live. When this future King comes into view, though, some may be surprised.

³ They see no chariot, no runners, no horses—and certainly no elephants. No, Jesus is riding on a lowly beast of burden, an ass.* No elaborate finery bedecks this rider

---

* In discussing this event, one reference work says that these animals "are lowly creatures," adding: "They are slow, stubborn, the perennial work animals of the poor, and not too handsome."

1-3. What is the manner of Jesus' entry into Jerusalem, and why might some in the crowd of onlookers be surprised?

or his mount. Instead of an expensive saddle, there are some garments that Jesus' close followers have spread over the animal's back. Why does Jesus choose to enter Jerusalem in such a lowly manner, when far lesser men have insisted on far greater pomp and ceremony?

⁴ Jesus is fulfilling a prophecy: "Be very joyful . . . Shout in triumph, O daughter of Jerusalem. Look! Your king himself comes to you. He is righteous, yes, saved; humble, and riding upon an ass." (Zechariah 9:9) This prophecy showed that God's Anointed One, the Messiah, would one day reveal himself to the people of Jerusalem as the divinely appointed King. Further, his very manner of doing so, including his choice of a mount, would reveal a beautiful quality of his heart —humility.

⁵ Jesus' humility is among his most appealing qualities, one that is soul-stirring to contemplate. As we discussed in the preceding chapter, Jesus alone is "the way and the truth and the life." (John 14:6) Clearly, none of the many billions of humans who have walked this earth has been nearly as important as God's Son. Yet, Jesus never showed so much as a trace of the pride, the haughtiness, or the self-importance that afflicts countless imperfect humans. To be followers of Christ, we need to fight the tendency to give in to pride. (James 4:6) Remember, Jehovah hates haughtiness. It is vital, then, that we learn to imitate Jesus' humility.

---

4. What did the Bible foretell about the manner in which the Messianic King would enter Jerusalem?
5. Why is Jesus' humility soul-stirring to contemplate, and why is it vital that we learn to imitate Jesus in this regard?

"Look! Your king himself comes to you"

A Long History of Showing Humility

⁶ Humility is lowliness of mind, an absence of haughtiness or pride. It is a quality that begins in the heart and is manifest in a person's speech, conduct, and dealings with others. How did Jehovah know that the Messiah would be humble? He knew that his Son reflected his own perfect example of humility. (John 10:15) He had also seen the Son's humility in action. How so?

⁷ The book of Jude reveals a fascinating example: "When Michael the archangel had a difference with the Devil and was disputing about Moses' body, he did not dare to bring a judgment against him in abusive terms, but said: 'May Jehovah rebuke you.'" (Jude 9) Michael is a name applied to Jesus—before and after his life on earth—in his role as archangel, or chief of Jehovah's heavenly army of angels.* (1 Thessalonians 4:16) Note, though, how Michael handled this confrontation with Satan.

⁸ Jude's account does not tell us what Satan wanted to do with Moses' body, but we can be sure that the Devil had some vile purpose in mind. Perhaps he wanted to promote the misuse of that faithful man's remains in false worship. While Michael resisted Satan's wicked scheme, he also showed remarkable self-restraint. Satan surely deserved a rebuke, but Michael, who at the time he was disputing with Satan had not yet had "all the judging" committed to him, felt that such a judgment should come

---

* For more evidence that Michael is Jesus, see pages 218-19 of the book *What Does the Bible Really Teach?* published by Jehovah's Witnesses.

---

6. What is humility, and how did Jehovah know that the Messiah would be humble?
7-9. (a) How did Michael display humility in his confrontation with Satan? (b) How might Christians imitate Michael in showing humility?

only from Jehovah God. (John 5:22) As archangel, Michael had extensive authority. Yet, he humbly deferred to Jehovah rather than trying to seize additional authority. Besides humility, he also showed modesty, or an awareness of his limitations.

⁹ Jude was inspired to write about this incident for a reason. Sadly, some Christians in Jude's day were not humble. They were haughtily "speaking abusively of all the things they really [did] not know." (Jude 10) How easy it is for us imperfect humans to let our pride get the better of us! When we do not understand something that is done in the Christian congregation—perhaps involving a decision made by the body of elders—how do we react? If we were to engage in negative, critical talk even though we cannot know all the factors behind such decisions, might we not be showing a lack of humility? Let us instead imitate Michael, or Jesus, holding back from judging matters over which we have no God-given authority.

¹⁰ God's Son also showed humility by accepting the assignment to come to earth. Consider what he had to leave behind. He was the archangel. He was also "the Word" —Jehovah's own Spokesman. (John 1:1-3) He resided in heaven, Jehovah's "lofty abode of holiness and beauty." (Isaiah 63:15) Nonetheless, the Son "emptied himself and took a slave's form and came to be in the likeness of men." (Philippians 2:7) Think of what his earthly assignment involved! His life was transferred to the womb of a Jewish virgin, there to develop for nine months to become a human baby. He was born a helpless infant into the household of a poor carpenter and then grew to be a toddler, a little boy, and a teenager. Although perfect

---

10, 11. (a) What is remarkable about the willingness of God's Son to accept the assignment to come to earth? (b) How might we imitate Jesus' humility?

himself, throughout his youth he remained subject to imperfect human parents. (Luke 2:40, 51, 52) What extraordinary humility!

[11] Can we imitate Jesus' humility by willingly accepting assignments of service that at times seem lowly? For example, our assignment to preach the good news of God's Kingdom may seem lowly when people respond with apathy, ridicule, or hostility. (Matthew 28:19, 20) If we endure in this work, though, we may help to save lives. At any rate, we will learn a great deal about humility, and we will follow in the footsteps of our Master, Jesus Christ.

Jesus' Humility as a Man

[12] From beginning to end, Jesus' earthly ministry was marked by humility. He showed it in the way he directed all praise and glory to his Father. People at times praised Jesus for the wisdom of his words, the power of his miracles, even the goodness of his character. Again and again, Jesus deflected such glory from himself and directed it to Jehovah.—Mark 10:17, 18; John 7:15, 16.

[13] Jesus showed humility in the way he treated people. In fact, he made it clear that he came to earth, not to be served, but to serve others. (Matthew 20:28) He showed humility in his mild, reasonable dealings with people. When his followers let him down, he did not berate them; he kept trying to reach their hearts. (Matthew 26:39-41) When the crowds interrupted his search for quiet, rest, and privacy, he did not send them away; he continued to give of himself, teaching them "many things." (Mark 6:30-34) When a non-Israelite woman kept begging him to heal her daughter, he initially indicated that he was not

_____

12-14. (a) How did Jesus show humility when people praised him? (b) In what ways did Jesus deal humbly with others? (c) What shows that Jesus' humility was not just a matter of form or good manners?

inclined to do so. However, he did not angrily refuse; he yielded in the light of her extraordinary faith, as we will discuss in Chapter 14.—Matthew 15:22-28.

[14] In countless ways, Jesus lived up to his own words about himself: "I am mild-tempered and lowly in heart." (Matthew 11:29) His humility was not superficial, a mere matter of form or good manners. It came from the heart, his inner self. No wonder, then, that Jesus placed high priority on teaching his followers to be humble!

Teaching His Followers to Be Humble

[15] Jesus' apostles were slow to cultivate humility. Jesus was compelled to try again and again to reach them. For example, on one occasion James and John through their mother asked Jesus to promise them elevated positions in God's Kingdom. Modestly, Jesus replied: "This sitting down at my right hand and at my left is not mine to give, but it belongs to those for whom it has been prepared by my Father." The ten other apostles were "indignant" at James and John. (Matthew 20:20-24) How did Jesus handle this problem?

[16] He kindly reprimanded them all, saying: "You know that the rulers of the nations lord it over them and the great men wield authority over them. This is not the way among you; but whoever wants to become great among you must be your minister, and whoever wants to be first among you must be your slave." (Matthew 20:25-27) The apostles had likely seen just how proud, ambitious, and selfish "the rulers of the nations" could be. Jesus showed that his followers must be different from those power-hungry tyrants. They needed to be humble. Did the apostles get the point?

15, 16. What contrast did Jesus note regarding the attitude of worldly rulers and the attitude that his followers needed to cultivate?

¹⁷ It was not easy for them. This was neither the first time nor the last time that Jesus taught such a lesson. Earlier, when they had argued over which one of them was the greatest, he had set a little child in their midst and told them to be more like children, who tend to lack the pride, ambition, and concern over rank that are so common in adults. (Matthew 18:1-4) Nonetheless, on the very eve of his death, he saw that his apostles were still struggling with pride. He then taught them a very memorable lesson. He girded himself with a towel and performed the lowliest of duties, one that servants back then commonly performed for household guests. Jesus washed the feet of each one of his apostles—including Judas, who was about to betray him!—John 13:1-11.

¹⁸ Jesus drove the point home when he told them: "I set the pattern for you." (John 13:15) Did this lesson finally reach their hearts? Well, later that night, they had yet another argument as to who was greatest among them! (Luke 22:24-27) Still, Jesus continued to be patient with them and taught them humbly. Then he went on to give the most powerful lesson of all: "He humbled himself and became obedient as far as death, yes, death on a torture stake." (Philippians 2:8) Jesus willingly submitted to a humiliating death, wrongly condemned as a criminal and a blasphemer. God's Son thereby proved unique, for in him among all of Jehovah's creatures humility found its perfect, its ultimate, expression.

¹⁹ Perhaps it was this—the final lesson in humility that Jesus taught as a man—that engraved the subject so indelibly in the hearts of his faithful apostles. The Bible tells us

---

17-19. (a) On the eve of his death, in what memorable way did Jesus teach his apostles a lesson about humility? (b) What was the most powerful lesson in humility that Jesus taught as a man?

that these men were humbly at work years, even decades, later. What about us?

Will You Follow the Pattern Jesus Set?

[20] Paul admonishes each of us: "Keep this mental attitude in you that was also in Christ Jesus." (Philippians 2:5) Like Jesus, we need to be lowly in heart. How can we know whether humility is in our heart? Well, Paul reminds us that we should be "doing nothing out of contentiousness or out of egotism, but with lowliness of mind considering that the others are superior to you." (Philippians 2:3) The key, then, lies in the way we view others in relation to ourselves. We need to see them as superior, as more important, than we are. Will you apply that counsel?

[21] Many years after Jesus' death, the apostle Peter was still thinking about the importance of humility. Peter taught Christian overseers to carry out their duties humbly, never lording it over Jehovah's sheep. (1 Peter 5:2, 3) Responsibility is no license for pride. On the contrary, responsibility increases the need for genuine humility. (Luke 12:48) Of course, this quality is vital not only for overseers but for every Christian.

[22] Peter surely never forgot that night when Jesus had washed his feet—over Peter's own objections! (John 13:6-10) Peter wrote to Christians: "All of you gird yourselves with lowliness of mind toward one another." (1 Peter 5:5) The expression "gird yourselves" suggests the action of a servant who would gird himself with an apron to carry out menial work. The phrase might well remind us of the occasion when Jesus girded himself with a towel before

---

20. How can we know whether we are lowly in heart?
21, 22. (a) Why do Christian overseers need to be humble? (b) How can we show that we are girded with humility?

How Can You Follow Jesus?

• When you are tempted to boast about your accomplishments, how might Jesus' example guide you?—Matthew 12:15-19; Mark 7:35-37.

• How might you imitate Jesus' example in doing humble work in behalf of spiritual brothers and sisters?—John 21: 1-13.

• How might you benefit from Jesus' example if you are tempted to seek prominence and success in this system of things? —John 6:14, 15.

---

kneeling to perform his task of washing feet. If we follow Jesus, what God-given assignment could we possibly consider beneath our dignity? The humility of our heart should be visible to all, as if we were girded with it.

²³ Haughtiness is like poison. The effects can be devastating. It is a quality that can render the most gifted human useless to God. Humility, on the other hand, can make even the least one very useful to Jehovah. If we cultivate this precious quality daily by endeavoring to walk humbly in the footsteps of Christ, the reward is wonderful to contemplate. Peter wrote: "Humble yourselves, therefore, under the mighty hand of God, that he may exalt you in due time." (1 Peter 5:6) Jehovah certainly exalted Jesus for humbling himself so completely. Our God will likewise delight in rewarding you for your humility.

²⁴ Sadly, some think that humility is a sign of weakness. Jesus' example helps us to see how false that notion is, for the humblest of men was also the most courageous. That will be the subject of the following chapter.

23, 24. (a) Why should we resist any tendency toward haughtiness? (b) The following chapter will help to correct what false notion regarding humility?

CHAPTER 4

"Look! The Lion That Is of the Tribe of Judah"

A MOB is coming after Jesus. Armed with swords and clubs and with soldiers among them, the men form a large crowd. As if guided by a single malevolent will, they move through the darkened streets of Jerusalem and across the Kidron Valley to the Mount of Olives. The moon is full, yet they carry torches and lamps. Do they light their way because clouds block the moonlight? Or do they expect their quarry to be hiding in the shadows? One thing is certain: Anyone who expects Jesus to cower knows little of the man.

2 Jesus is aware of the danger that approaches. Nonetheless, he stands and waits. The mob nears, led by Judas, once a trusted friend. Judas brazenly betrays Jesus, singling out his former master with a hypocritical greeting and a kiss. Still, Jesus keeps his composure. Then he steps out before the mob. "Whom are you looking for?" he asks. "Jesus the Nazarene," they reply.

3 Most people would quail in terror before such an armed mob. Perhaps that is what this crowd expects of the man before them. But Jesus does not cower, does not flee, does not blurt out some lie. Instead, he simply says: "I am he." His manner is so calm, so brave, that the men are astounded. They stagger backward and fall down! —John 18:1-6; Matthew 26:45-50; Mark 14:41-46.

4 How could Jesus face such extreme danger with

1-3. What danger comes upon Jesus, and how does he react?
4-6. (a) God's Son is likened to what, and why? (b) What are three ways in which Jesus displayed courage?

complete composure and self-restraint? The answer, in a word, is courage. Few qualities are so admired or so needed in a leader, and no man has ever equaled, much less excelled, Jesus in this regard. In the preceding chapter, we learned how humble and meek Jesus was. He was rightly called "the Lamb." (John 1:29) Jesus' courage, however, gives rise to a very different description. The Bible says of God's Son: "Look! The Lion that is of the tribe of Judah." —Revelation 5:5.

[5] The lion is often linked to courage. Have you ever stood face-to-face with an adult male lion? If you have, most likely you were safely separated from the beast, perhaps by the fence of his enclosure at a zoo. Still, such an experience can be daunting. As you look into the face of this huge and powerful creature and he gazes steadily back at you, you can hardly imagine the lion ever fleeing in fear from anything. The Bible speaks of "the lion, which is the mightiest among the beasts and which does not turn back from before anyone." (Proverbs 30:30) Such is the courage of Christ.

[6] Let us discuss how Jesus displayed lionlike courage in three ways: in standing up for the truth, in upholding justice, and in facing opposition. We will see, too, that all of us—whether naturally brave or not—can imitate Jesus in showing courage.

He Courageously Stood Up for the Truth

[7] In a world ruled by Satan, "the father of the lie," it often takes courage to stand up for the truth. (John 8:44; 14:30) Jesus did not wait until adulthood before taking such a stand. When 12 years old, Jesus was separated from his

7-9. (a) What happened when Jesus was 12 years old, and what strikes you as intimidating about that situation? (b) How did Jesus display courage in dealing with the teachers in the temple?

parents after the Passover festival in Jerusalem. For three days, Mary and Joseph searched frantically for the boy. They finally found him in the temple. And what was he doing there? "Sitting in the midst of the teachers and listening to them and questioning them." (Luke 2:41-50) Consider the setting for that discussion.

[8] Historians say that some of the foremost religious leaders would customarily remain at the temple after festivals and teach at one of the spacious porches there. People would sit at their feet to listen and to ask questions. These teachers were learned men. They were well versed in the Mosaic Law and also in the endlessly complex manmade laws and traditions that had multiplied over the years. How might you have felt sitting in their midst? Intimidated? That would be only natural. And what if you were just 12 years old? Many young ones are shy. (Jeremiah 1:6) Some try desperately to avoid attracting the attention of their teachers in school; these youths fear being called on, fear being singled out, fear the possibility of being embarrassed or ridiculed.

[9] Yet, here we find Jesus, sitting in the midst of those learned men, fearlessly asking them probing questions. And he did still more. The account tells us: "All those listening to him were in constant amazement at his understanding and his answers." (Luke 2:47) The Bible does not tell us what he said on that occasion, but we can be confident that he did not parrot the falsehoods that were so favored among those religious teachers. (1 Peter 2:22) No, he upheld the truth of God's Word, and his listeners were surely amazed that a 12-year-old boy could express himself with such insight and courage.

[10] Today, countless young Christians are following in

---

10. How do young Christians today imitate Jesus' courage?

Jesus' footsteps. Granted, they are not perfect, as young Jesus was. Like him, though, they do not wait to reach adulthood before standing up for the truth. At school or in the communities where they live, they tactfully ask people questions, listen, and respectfully share with them the truth. (1 Peter 3:15) As a group, these young ones have helped classmates, teachers, and neighbors to become followers of Christ. How their courage must please Jehovah! His Word likens such youths to dewdrops—refreshing, pleasing, and numerous.—Psalm 110:3.

[11] In manhood, Jesus showed courage again and again in defending the truth. In fact, his ministry opened with a confrontation that many would call terrifying. Not as the mighty archangel, but as a mere man of flesh and blood, Jesus had to face Satan, the most powerful and dangerous of all of Jehovah's enemies. Jesus rejected Satan and refuted his misapplication of inspired Scripture. Jesus ended the encounter by commanding boldly: "Go away, Satan!" —Matthew 4:2-11.

[12] Jesus thus set the pattern for his ministry, bravely defending his Father's Word against efforts to twist it or misuse it. Then, as now, such religious dishonesty was all too common. Jesus told religious leaders of his day: "You make the word of God invalid by your tradition which you handed down." (Mark 7:13) Those men were greatly revered by the people in general, but Jesus fearlessly denounced them as blind guides and hypocrites.* (Matthew

---

* Historians have noted that the tombs of the rabbis were venerated in much the same way as were the tombs of prophets and patriarchs.

11, 12. As an adult, how did Jesus show courage in defending the truth?

23:13, 16) How can we imitate this aspect of Jesus' courageous example?

Many Christian youths courageously share their faith with others

[13] We remember, of course, that we have neither Jesus' ability to read hearts nor his authority to judge. However, we can imitate his bold defense of the truth. For example, by exposing religious falsehoods—the lies so often taught about God, his purposes, and his Word—we shed light in a world bedarkened by Satan's propaganda. (Matthew 5:14; Revelation 12:9, 10) We help to free people from enslavement to false teachings that fill their hearts with morbid fear and that poison their relationship with God. What a privilege we have to see the fulfillment of Jesus' promise: "The truth will set you free"!—John 8:32.

He Courageously Upheld Justice

[14] Bible prophecy foretold that the Messiah would clarify to the nations "what justice is." (Matthew 12:18; Isaiah 42:1) Jesus certainly began to do so while here on earth. With great courage, he proved ever just and impartial in his dealings with people. For example, he refused to adopt

---

13. What do we need to remember in imitating Jesus, yet what privilege do we have?
14, 15. (a) What is one way in which Jesus made clear "what justice is"? (b) In speaking to a Samaritan woman, what prejudices did Jesus ignore?

the unscriptural prejudices and bigotry that were so prevalent in the world around him.

¹⁵ When Jesus spoke to a Samaritan woman at the well of Sychar, his disciples were surprised. Why? In those days, the Jews in general detested the Samaritans; this disdain reached back many, many years. (Ezra 4:4) Furthermore, some rabbis held a disparaging view of women. The rabbinic rules, later put into writing, discouraged a man from conversing with a woman; they even suggested that women were unworthy of being taught God's Law. Samaritan women in particular were viewed as unclean. Jesus ignored such unjust prejudices and openly taught the Samaritan woman (who was living an immoral life), even revealing to her his identity as the Messiah.—John 4:5-27.

¹⁶ Have you ever found yourself in company with those who harbor ugly prejudices? Perhaps they joke contemptuously about people of another race or nation, speak disparagingly about members of the opposite sex, or look down on those of a different economic or social status. Followers of Christ do not sympathize with such hateful views, and they work hard to eradicate any trace of prejudice in their own hearts. (Acts 10:34) Each of us needs to cultivate the courage to be just in this regard.

¹⁷ Courage also led Jesus to fight for the cleanness of God's people and for the arrangement for pure worship. Early in his ministry, he entered the temple area in Jerusalem and was appalled to see merchants and money changers operating their businesses there. Filled with righteous indignation, Jesus threw those greedy men and their merchandise out of there. (John 2:13-17) He took similar ac-

---

16. Why do Christians need the courage to be different when it comes to prejudice?
17. What action did Jesus take in the temple, and why?

tion later, near the close of his ministry. (Mark 11:15-18) These deeds surely made him some powerful enemies, yet he did not hesitate. Why? From childhood, he called that temple his Father's house—and he meant it. (Luke 2:49) To pollute the pure worship carried on there was an injustice he could never condone. His zeal gave him the courage to do what was needed.

[18] Christ's followers today likewise care deeply about the cleanness of God's people and the arrangement for pure worship. If they see that a fellow Christian is involved in serious wrongdoing, they do not simply turn a blind eye. They courageously speak up. (1 Corinthians 1:11) They make sure that the congregation elders are informed. The elders can help those who are spiritually sick and can also take action to preserve the clean standing of Jehovah's sheep.—James 5:14, 15.

[19] Should we conclude, though, that Jesus fought social injustice in the world at large? There certainly were injustices all around him. His homeland was occupied by a foreign power. The Romans oppressed the Jews with a powerful military presence, taxed them heavily, and even interfered with their religious customs. Not surprisingly, many people wanted Jesus to get involved in the politics of his day. (John 6:14, 15) Again, his courage had to come into play.

[20] Jesus explained that his Kingdom was no part of the world. By his example, he trained his followers to keep out of the political fights of the day and to focus instead on

18. How may Christians today show courage when it comes to the cleanness of the congregation?
19, 20. (a) What injustices were rampant in Jesus' day, and what pressure did Jesus face? (b) Why do Christ's followers refuse to get involved in politics and violence, and what is one reward for their stand?

preaching the good news of God's Kingdom. (John 17:16; 18:36) He taught a powerful lesson regarding neutrality when the mob came to arrest him. Peter sprang into action, impulsively swinging his sword and injuring a man. It is easy to sympathize with Peter. If ever violence might have seemed justified, it was on that night, when God's innocent Son was attacked. Yet, Jesus then set the standard for his earthly followers down to this day: "Return your sword to its place, for all those who take the sword will perish by the sword." (Matthew 26:51-54) For Christ's followers, maintaining such a peaceful stand surely took courage then, as it does today. As a result of their Christian neutrality, God's people today have a clean record when it comes to the countless modern-day wars, holocausts, riots, and similar acts of violence. That sterling record is one reward for their courage.

He Courageously Faced Opposition

21 Jehovah's Son knew well in advance that he would face severe opposition when here on earth. (Isaiah 50: 4-7) He faced many threats of death, culminating in the one described at the outset of this chapter. How did Jesus maintain his courage in the face of such dangers? Well, what was Jesus doing before that mob came to arrest him? He was praying fervently to Jehovah. And what did Jehovah do? The Bible tells us that Jesus "was favorably heard." (Hebrews 5:7) Jehovah sent an angel from heaven to strengthen his brave Son.—Luke 22:42, 43.

22 Shortly after being strengthened, Jesus said to his apostles: "Get up, let us go." (Matthew 26:46) Think of

21, 22. (a) Jesus received what help before facing the hardest of his trials? (b) How did Jesus prove courageous to the end?

"I am he"

the bravery in those words. "Let us go," he said, knowing that he would ask the mob to spare his friends, knowing that those companions would abandon him and flee, and knowing that he would go on alone to face the hardest ordeal of his life. Alone, he faced an illegal and unjust trial, ridicule, torture, and an agonizing death. Throughout it all, his courage never failed him.

²³ Was Jesus being reckless? No; recklessness has little to do with true courage. In fact, Jesus taught his followers to be cautious, to withdraw prudently from danger in or-

---

23. Explain why Jesus was not reckless in the way that he faced danger and the threat of death.

*Jehovah's Witnesses have shown courage
in the face of persecution*

How Can You Follow Jesus?

• How can Jesus' example help you to speak courageously, even if people find the truths you share offensive?—John 8: 31-59.

• Why should we never let a morbid dread of Satan or his demons hold us back from helping others?—Matthew 8:28-34; Mark 1:23-28.

• Why should we be willing to risk persecution in order to show compassion for the downtrodden?—John 9:1, 6, 7, 22-41.

• How did Jesus' hope for the future help him to face trials, and how can your hope give you courage?—John 16:28; 17:5; Hebrews 12:2.

der to continue doing God's will. (Matthew 4:12; 10:16) In this case, though, Jesus knew that there was no way to withdraw. He knew what God's will involved. Jesus was determined to keep his integrity, so the only way to go was forward, right into the trial.

24 How often Jesus' followers have walked courageously in their Master's footsteps! Many have stood firm in the face of ridicule, persecution, arrest, imprisonment, torture, and even death. Where do imperfect humans get such courage? It does not simply arise from within. As Jesus received help from above, so do his followers. (Philippians 4:13) Never fear, then, what the future may bring. Be determined to keep your integrity, and Jehovah will give you the courage you need. Keep drawing strength from the example of our Leader, Jesus, who said: "Take courage! I have conquered the world."—John 16:33.

---

24. Why may we be assured that we can prove courageous in the face of any trial that may arise?

CHAPTER 5

"All the Treasures of Wisdom"

IT IS a spring day in 31 C.E. Jesus Christ is near Capernaum, a bustling city on the northwest shores of the Sea of Galilee. Up on a mountain in the vicinity, Jesus has prayed in solitude the entire night. As the morning unfolds, he calls his disciples, and from among them he chooses 12, whom he names apostles. Meanwhile, great crowds of people—some from considerable distances—have followed Jesus to this location and are assembled at a level place on the mountain. They are eager to hear what he has to say and to be healed of their ailments. Jesus does not disappoint them.—Luke 6:12-19.

2 Jesus approaches the crowds and heals all who are sick. Finally, when not one among them feels the pain of serious illness, he sits down and begins to teach.* His words spoken in the spring air that day must surprise his listeners. After all, they have never heard anyone teach as he does. To give weight to his teachings, he appeals neither to oral traditions nor to well-known Jewish rabbis. Rather, he repeatedly quotes the inspired Hebrew Scriptures. His message is straightforward, his wording simple, his meaning clear. When he is finished, the crowds are astounded.

---

* The discourse Jesus delivered that day has come to be known as the Sermon on the Mount. As recorded at Matthew 5:3–7:27, it contains 107 verses and would likely take just 20 minutes or so to deliver.

1-3. What is the setting for the sermon that Jesus delivers on a spring day in 31 C.E., and why are his listeners astounded?

Indeed, they should be. They have just listened to the wisest man who ever lived!—Matthew 7:28, 29.

³ That sermon along with many other things that Jesus said and did is recorded in God's Word. We do well to dig into what that inspired record says about Jesus, for in him are "all the treasures of wisdom." (Colossians 2:3) Where did he get such wisdom—the ability to put knowledge and understanding to work in a practical way? How did he manifest wisdom, and how can we follow his example?

"Where Did This Man Get This Wisdom?"

⁴ During one of his preaching tours, Jesus visited Nazareth, the town where he had been reared, and began teaching in the synagogue there. Many of his listeners were amazed and wondered: "Where did this man get this wisdom?" They knew his family—his parents and siblings—and they were aware that he had come from humble circumstances. (Matthew 13:54-56; Mark 6:1-3) They no doubt also knew that this eloquent carpenter had not attended any of the prestigious rabbinic schools. (John 7: 15) Their question thus seemed logical.

⁵ The wisdom Jesus manifested was not simply the product of his perfect mind. Later in his ministry, when teaching openly in the temple, Jesus revealed that his wisdom was from a far loftier source. "What I teach is not mine," he said, "but belongs to him that sent me." (John 7: 16) Yes, the Father, who sent forth the Son, was the real source of Jesus' wisdom. (John 12:49) How, though, did Jesus receive wisdom from Jehovah?

⁶ Jehovah's holy spirit was at work in Jesus' heart and mind. Concerning Jesus as the promised Messiah, Isa-

4. What question did Jesus' listeners in Nazareth raise, and why?
5. Jesus revealed that his wisdom was from what source?
6, 7. In what ways did Jesus receive wisdom from his Father?

iah foretold: "Upon him the spirit of Jehovah must settle down, the spirit of wisdom and of understanding, the spirit of counsel and of mightiness, the spirit of knowledge and of the fear of Jehovah." (Isaiah 11:2) With Jehovah's spirit resting upon him and guiding his thinking and decisions, is it any wonder that Jesus' words and actions reflected superlative wisdom?

7 Jesus gained wisdom from his Father in another profound way. As we saw in Chapter 2, during his prehuman existence, which spanned countless ages, Jesus had the opportunity to absorb his Father's thoughts on matters. We cannot begin to imagine the depth of wisdom that the Son gained at his Father's side, laboring as God's "master worker" in the creation of all other things, both animate and inanimate. For good reason, the Son in his prehuman existence is described as wisdom personified. (Proverbs 8:22-31; Colossians 1:15, 16) Throughout his ministry, Jesus was able to draw on the wisdom he had gained alongside his Father in heaven.* (John 8:26, 28, 38) Therefore, we need hardly be surprised at the breadth of knowledge and depth of understanding reflected in Jesus' words or at the soundness of judgment evident in his every deed.

8 As followers of Jesus, we too need to look to Jehovah as the source of wisdom. (Proverbs 2:6) Of course, Jehovah does not impart miraculous wisdom to us. He does, however, answer our earnest prayers for the wisdom necessary to deal successfully with the challenges of life. (James 1:5) To gain that wisdom requires much effort on our part. We

---

* Evidently, when "the heavens were opened up" at the time of Jesus' baptism, the memory of his prehuman existence was restored to him.—Matthew 3:13-17.

8. As followers of Jesus, how may we gain wisdom?

need to keep seeking for it "as for hid treasures." (Proverbs 2:1-6) Yes, we need to continue digging deep down into God's Word, wherein his wisdom is revealed, and to bring our life into harmony with what we learn. The example of Jehovah's Son is especially valuable in helping us to acquire wisdom. Let us examine several areas in which Jesus manifested wisdom and learn how we can imitate him.

Words of Wisdom

9 People in great numbers flocked to Jesus just to hear him speak. (Mark 6:31-34; Luke 5:1-3) And no wonder, for when Jesus opened his mouth, words of surpassing wisdom issued forth! His teachings reflected a deep knowledge of God's Word and a matchless ability to get to the heart of matters. His teachings are universal in their appeal and timeless in their application. Consider some examples of the wisdom found in the words of Jesus, the foretold "Wonderful Counselor."—Isaiah 9:6.

10 The Sermon on the Mount, referred to at the outset, is the largest collection of Jesus' teachings not interrupted by narrative or the words of others. In this sermon, Jesus does not simply ad-

9. What made Jesus' teachings so wise?
10. What positive qualities does Jesus urge us to cultivate, and why?

God's wisdom is revealed in the Bible

vise us to pursue proper speech and conduct. His counsel goes much deeper than that. Well aware that thoughts and feelings lead to words and actions, Jesus urges us to cultivate positive qualities of mind and heart, such as mildness of temper, a hunger for righteousness, an inclination to be merciful and peaceable, and love for others. (Matthew 5:5-9, 43-48) As we build up such qualities in our heart, the result will be wholesome speech and conduct that not only please Jehovah but also promote good relationships with fellow humans.—Matthew 5:16.

11 When giving counsel on sinful behavior, Jesus gets to the very root of the matter. He does not simply tell us to refrain from violent acts. Rather, he warns us not to allow anger to smolder in our heart. (Matthew 5:21, 22; 1 John 3:15) He does not only forbid the act of adultery. Instead, he warns of the passion that begins in the heart and leads to such betrayal. He admonishes us not to allow our eyes to arouse improper desire and stimulate lust. (Matthew 5: 27-30) Jesus deals with causes, not just symptoms. He addresses the attitudes and desires that give birth to sinful deeds.—Psalm 7:14.

12 What wisdom there is in the words of Jesus! Little wonder that "the crowds were astounded at his way of teaching." (Matthew 7:28) As his followers, we view his wise counsel as a pattern for living. We seek to cultivate the positive qualities he recommended—including mercy, peaceableness, and love—knowing that we will thus be laying a foundation for godly conduct. We endeavor to root out of our heart the negative feelings and desires he warned against, such as bitter anger and immoral

---

11. When giving counsel on sinful behavior, how does Jesus get to the root of the matter?

12. How do followers of Jesus view his counsel, and why?

longings, knowing that doing so will help us to avoid sinful conduct.—James 1:14, 15.

A Way of Life Governed by Wisdom

13 Jesus manifested wisdom not only in word but also in deed. His entire manner of life—his decisions, his view of himself, and his dealings with others—demonstrated wisdom in its many beautiful facets. Consider some examples showing that Jesus was governed by "practical wisdom and thinking ability."—Proverbs 3:21.

14 Wisdom includes sound judgment. *Jesus used good judgment in choosing his life course.* Can you imagine the life that he could have made for himself—the home he could have constructed, the business he could have built up, or the worldly prominence he could have achieved? Jesus knew that a life devoted to those pursuits "is vanity and a striving after the wind." (Ecclesiastes 4:4; 5:10) Such a course is foolishness, the opposite of wisdom. Jesus chose to keep his life simple. He was not interested in making money or accumulating material possessions. (Matthew 8:20) In line with what he taught, he kept his eye focused on a single purpose—the doing of God's will. (Matthew 6:22) Jesus wisely devoted his time and energy to Kingdom interests, which are far more important and rewarding than material things. (Matthew 6:19-21) He thus left behind an example worthy of imitation.

15 Followers of Jesus today see the wisdom of keeping a simple eye. They therefore avoid weighing themselves down with unnecessary debt and with mundane pursuits that consume too much attention and energy. (1 Timothy

13, 14. What shows that Jesus used good judgment in choosing his life course?

15. How can followers of Jesus demonstrate that they are keeping a simple eye, and why is this the course of wisdom?

6:9, 10) Many have taken steps to simplify their lifestyle so that they can devote more time to the Christian ministry, perhaps even serving as full-time Kingdom proclaimers. There could hardly be a wiser course to pursue, for keeping Kingdom interests in their rightful place results in the greatest happiness and satisfaction.—Matthew 6:33.

16 The Bible associates wisdom with modesty, which includes being aware of our limitations. (Proverbs 11:2) *Jesus was modest and realistic in what he expected of himself.* He knew that he was not going to convert everyone who heard his message. (Matthew 10:32-39) He also realized that there was a limit to the number of people that he would personally be able to reach. So he wisely entrusted the disciple-making work to his followers. (Matthew 28:18-20) He modestly acknowledged that they would "do works greater than" his own, for they would reach more people over a greater area and for a longer period of time. (John 14:12) Jesus also recognized that he was not beyond needing help. He accepted the aid of the angels who came to minister to him in the wilderness and of the angel who came to strengthen him in Gethsemane. In his moment of greatest need, the Son of God cried out for help.—Matthew 4:11; Luke 22:43; Hebrews 5:7.

17 We too need to be modest and realistic in what we expect of ourselves. We certainly want to work wholesouled and to exert ourselves vigorously in the preaching and disciple-making work. (Luke 13:24; Colossians 3: 23) At the same time, we need to remember that Jehovah does not compare us with one another, nor should we. (Galatians 6:4) Practical wisdom will help us to set realistic goals in accord with our abilities and circumstances. In

16, 17. (a) In what ways did Jesus demonstrate that he was modest and realistic in what he expected of himself? (b) How may we show that we are modest and realistic in what we expect of ourselves?

addition, wisdom will guide those in positions of responsibility to acknowledge that they have limitations and that they need help and support from time to time. Modesty will enable such ones to accept the help graciously, recognizing that Jehovah may well use a fellow believer to become "a strengthening aid" to them.—Colossians 4:11.

[18] "The wisdom from above is . . . reasonable," says James 3:17. *Jesus was reasonable and positive in dealing with his disciples.* He was well aware of their faults, yet he looked for the good in them. (John 1:47) He knew that they were going to abandon him on the night of his arrest, but he did not doubt their loyalty. (Matthew 26:31-35; Luke 22:28-30) Peter three times denied even knowing Jesus. Still, Jesus made supplication in Peter's behalf and expressed confidence in his faithfulness. (Luke 22:31-34) On the last night of his earthly life, Jesus in prayer to his Father did not focus on the mistakes his disciples had made. Rather, he spoke positively about their course up to that night, saying: "They have observed your word." (John 17:6) Despite their imperfections, he placed in their hands the earthly interests of his Kingdom. (Matthew 25:14, 15; Luke 12:42-44) The confidence and faith that he expressed in them no doubt strengthened them to carry out the work he commanded them to do.

[19] Followers of Jesus have reason to imitate his example in this regard. If the perfect Son of God was patient in dealing with his imperfect disciples, how much more should we as sinful humans be reasonable in our dealings with one another! (Philippians 4:5) Rather than focusing on the shortcomings of fellow worshippers, we do well to look for the good in them. We are wise to remem-

---

18, 19. (a) What shows that Jesus was reasonable and positive in dealing with his disciples? (b) Why do we have good reason to be positive and reasonable in dealing with one another, and how can we do so?

How Can You Follow Jesus?

• If you sense that you offended a fellow believer, what is the course of wisdom?—Matthew 5:23, 24.

• When you are insulted or provoked, how might Jesus' words help you to respond wisely?—Matthew 5:38-42.

• How could meditating on Jesus' words help you to keep a balanced view of money and possessions?—Matthew 6:24-34.

• When setting priorities in your life, how might following Jesus' example help you to make a wise decision?—Luke 4:43; John 4:34.

ber that Jehovah has drawn them. (John 6:44) Surely, then, he must see some measure of good in them, and so should we. A positive spirit will help us not only to "overlook faults" but also to search out areas in which we can commend others. (Proverbs 19:11, *The New English Bible*) When we express confidence in our Christian brothers and sisters, we help them to do their best in serving Jehovah and to find joy in that service.—1 Thessalonians 5:11.

[20] The Gospel accounts of Jesus' life and ministry truly are a treasure trove of wisdom! What should we do with this priceless gift? At the conclusion of the Sermon on the Mount, Jesus urged his audience not just to *hear* his wise sayings but also to *do,* or apply, them. (Matthew 7:24-27) Molding our thoughts, motivations, and actions according to Jesus' wise words and deeds will help us to find the best possible life now and to stay on the road to everlasting life. (Matthew 7:13, 14) Surely there is no better or wiser course that we could take!

---

20. What should we do with the treasure trove of wisdom found in the Gospel accounts, and why?

CHAPTER 6

"He Learned Obedience"

A FATHER looks out the window, watching his young son at play with some friends. Their ball bounces out of the yard and into the street. The boy looks longingly after it. One of his friends urges him to run out into the street to get it, but the boy shakes his head. "I'm not allowed to do that," he says. The father smiles to himself.

2 Why is the father so pleased? Because he has instructed his son not to go out into the street alone. When the boy obeys—even though he does not know that his father is watching—the father knows that his son is learning obedience and is much safer as a result. That father feels as does our heavenly Father, Jehovah. God knows that if we are to remain faithful and live to see the wonderful future he has in store for us, we must learn to trust in him and obey him. (Proverbs 3:5, 6) To that end, he sent us the best of all human teachers.

3 The Bible says something amazing about Jesus: "Although he was a Son, he learned obedience from the things he suffered; and after he had been made perfect he became responsible for everlasting salvation to all those obeying him." (Hebrews 5:8, 9) This Son had existed for countless ages in heaven. He saw Satan and his fellow rebel angels disobey, but the firstborn Son never joined them. Inspired prophecy applied these words to

1, 2. Why is a loving father pleased to see his son obey him, and how do his feelings reflect Jehovah's feelings?
3, 4. How is it that Jesus "learned obedience" and was "made perfect"? Illustrate.

him: "I . . . was not rebellious." (Isaiah 50:5) How, then, could the words "he learned obedience" apply to this perfectly obedient Son? How could such a perfect creature be "made perfect"?

⁴ Consider an illustration. A soldier has an iron sword. Although it has never been tested in battle, it is perfectly formed and well crafted. However, he trades that sword for one made of a stronger metal, hardened steel. This new sword has already served well in battle. Is that not a wise trade? Similarly, the obedience Jesus demonstrated before he came to the earth was flawless. But after his sojourn here, his obedience was of an altogether different quality. It was now tested, hardened, as it were, and proved by trials that Jesus could never have encountered in heaven.

⁵ Obedience was central to Jesus' mission in coming to the earth. As "the last Adam," Jesus came here to do what our first parent failed to do—remain obedient to Jehovah God, even under test. (1 Corinthians 15:45) Yet, Jesus' obedience was not mechanical. Jesus obeyed with all his mind, heart, and soul. And he did it with joy. Doing his Father's will was more important to him than was eating! (John 4:34) What will help us to imitate Jesus' obedience? Let us first consider his motives. Cultivating motives like his will help us both to resist temptation and to carry out God's will. We will then review some rewards that result from manifesting Christlike obedience.

Jesus' Motives for Obedience

⁶ Jesus' obedience stemmed from what was in his heart. As we saw in Chapter 3, Christ was humble at heart.

---

5. What made Jesus' obedience so important, and what will we consider in this chapter?
6, 7. What were some of Jesus' motives for obedience?

Arrogant pride makes people disdain obedience, whereas humility helps us to obey Jehovah willingly. (Exodus 5: 1, 2; 1 Peter 5:5, 6) Further, Jesus' obedience arose from what he loved and from what he hated.

⁷ Above all, Jesus loved his heavenly Father, Jehovah. That love will be discussed in greater detail in Chapter 13. Such love gave rise to Jesus' godly fear. So intense was his love for Jehovah, so profound his reverence, that he feared to displease his Father. Godly fear was one reason why Jesus' prayers were favorably heard. (Hebrews 5:7) Fear of Jehovah is also an outstanding mark of Jesus' rule as Messianic King.—Isaiah 11:3.

⁸ Love for Jehovah also involves hatred for what Jehovah

8, 9. As prophesied, how did Jesus feel about righteousness and wickedness, and how did he make those feelings evident?

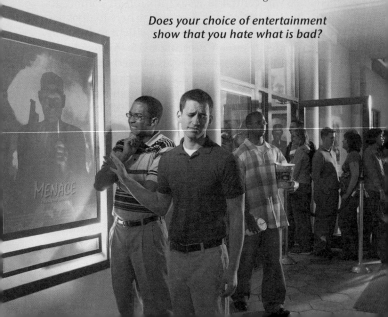

Does your choice of entertainment show that you hate what is bad?

hates. Note, for example, this prophecy addressed to the Messianic King: "You have loved righteousness and you hate wickedness. That is why God, your God, has anointed you with the oil of exultation more than your partners." (Psalm 45:7) Jesus' "partners" were the other kings in the family line of King David. More than any of them, Jesus has cause for exultation, or intense joy, at his anointing. Why? His reward is far greater than theirs, his kingship infinitely more beneficial. He is rewarded because his love of righteousness and hatred of wickedness moved him to obey God in all things.

9 How did Jesus make his feelings regarding righteousness and wickedness evident? For instance, when his followers obeyed his direction in the preaching work and were blessed as a result, how did Jesus react? He was overjoyed. (Luke 10:1, 17, 21) And when the people of Jerusalem repeatedly showed a disobedient spirit, rejecting his loving efforts to help them, how did Jesus feel? He wept because of that city's rebellious course. (Luke 19:41, 42) Jesus felt very deeply about conduct both good and bad.

10 Meditating on Jesus' feelings helps us to examine our own motives for obeying Jehovah. Imperfect though we are, we can cultivate a heartfelt love of good deeds and an earnest hatred of wrong conduct. We need to pray to Jehovah, asking him to help us to cultivate feelings that are like his and like those of his Son. (Psalm 51:10) At the same time, we need to avoid influences that will erode such feelings. Careful choices of entertainment and associations are essential. (Proverbs 13:20; Philippians 4:8) If we cultivate Christlike motives, our obedience will not be a mere formality. We will do what is right because we love

---

10. What feelings do we need to cultivate when it comes to righteous deeds and wrong acts, and what will help us do so?

to do it. We will avoid wrong deeds, not because we fear getting caught, but because we hate such conduct.

"He Committed No Sin"

[11] In regard to his hatred of sin, Jesus was tested early in his ministry. After his baptism, he spent 40 days and nights in the wilderness without food. At the end of that period, Satan came to tempt him. Note how crafty the Devil was.—Matthew 4:1-11.

[12] Satan first said: "If you are a son of God, tell these stones to become loaves of bread." (Matthew 4:3) How did Jesus feel after his long fast? The Bible plainly says: "He felt hungry." (Matthew 4:2) So Satan played on the natural desire for food, no doubt deliberately waiting until Jesus was in a physically weakened state. Notice, too, Satan's taunting phrase: *"If* you are a son of God." Satan knew that Jesus was "the firstborn of all creation." (Colossians 1:15) Still, Jesus did not allow Satan to provoke him into disobedience. Jesus knew that it was not God's will that he use his power for selfish ends. He refused to do so, showing that he humbly relied on Jehovah for sustenance and direction.—Matthew 4:4.

[13] For his second temptation, Satan took Jesus to a lofty spot on the temple battlement. Cleverly twisting God's Word, Satan tempted Jesus to make a showy display by hurling himself down from that height so that angels would have to rescue him. If the crowds at the temple saw such a miracle, would anyone thereafter dare raise a doubt that Jesus was the promised Messiah? And if the crowds

---

11, 12. (a) What happened to Jesus early in his ministry? (b) How did Satan first tempt Jesus, using what crafty tactics?
13-15. (a) What were Satan's second and third temptations of Jesus, and how did Jesus respond? (b) How do we know that Jesus was never able to let down his guard against Satan?

accepted Jesus as the Messiah on the basis of such show-manship, might Jesus not avoid a lot of hardship and trouble? Perhaps. But Jesus knew that it was Jehovah's will for the Messiah to carry out his work in a humble manner, not to influence people to believe in him by means of spectacular displays. (Isaiah 42:1, 2) Again, Jesus refused to disobey Jehovah. Fame held no lure for him.

14 What, though, about the lure of power? In his third attempt, Satan offered Jesus all the kingdoms of the world if Jesus would perform a single act of worship to Satan. Did he seriously consider Satan's offer? "Go away, Satan!" was his reply. He added: "For it is written, 'It is Jehovah your God you must worship, and it is to him alone you must render sacred service.'" (Matthew 4:10) Nothing would ever induce Jesus to worship another god. No offer of power or influence in this world would sway him to commit any act of disobedience.

15 Did Satan give up? He did leave at Jesus' command. However, Luke's Gospel states that the Devil "retired from him until another convenient time." (Luke 4:13) Indeed, Satan would find other occasions to test and to tempt Jesus, right down to the end. The Bible tells us that Jesus was "tested in all respects." (Hebrews 4:15) So Jesus was never able to let down his guard; nor are we.

16 Satan continues to tempt God's servants today. Sadly, our imperfections often make us easy targets. Satan craftily appeals to selfishness, pride, and greed for power. Using the lure of materialism, Satan may even appeal to all of these at once! It is vital that we pause, at times, for honest self-examination. We do well to meditate on the words of 1 John 2:15-17. As we do, we might ask ourselves

16. How does Satan tempt God's servants today, and how may we reject his efforts?

if the fleshly desires of this system of things, the yearning for material possessions, and the desire to impress others have to some extent eroded our love for our heavenly Father. We need to remember that this world is on its way out, as is its ruler, Satan. Let us reject his crafty efforts to lure us into sin! May we be inspired by our Master, for "he committed no sin."—1 Peter 2:22.

"I Always Do the Things Pleasing to Him"

¹⁷ Obedience involves far more than refraining from sin; Christ actively carried out his Father's every command. He declared: "I always do the things pleasing to him." (John 8:29) This obedience brought Jesus great joy. Of course, some might object that obedience was less complicated for Jesus. They might imagine that he had to answer only to Jehovah, who is perfect, whereas we often have to answer to imperfect humans in positions of authority. The truth is, though, that Jesus *was* obedient to imperfect humans who had positions of authority.

¹⁸ As he was growing up, Jesus was under the authority of his imperfect human parents, Joseph and Mary. Likely, more than most children, he could see flaws in his parents. Did he rebel, stepping out of his God-given role and telling them how to manage a family? Note what Luke 2:51 says of 12-year-old Jesus: "He continued subject to them." In this obedience, he set an excellent example for Christian youths, who strive to obey their parents and show them due respect.—Ephesians 6:1, 2.

¹⁹ When it comes to obeying imperfect humans, Jesus

---

17. How did Jesus feel about obeying his Father, yet what objection may some raise?
18. As a youth, Jesus set what example in obedience?
19, 20. (a) Jesus faced what unique challenges regarding obedience to imperfect humans? (b) Why should true Christians today be obedient to those taking the lead among them?

*We obediently apply what we learn
at Christian meetings*

faced challenges that true Christians today never have to face. Consider the unique times in which he lived. The Jewish religious system of things, with its temple in Jerusalem and its priesthood, had long been approved by Jehovah but was about to be cast off and replaced with the Christian congregation arrangement. (Matthew 23:33-38) Meanwhile, many of the religious leaders were teaching falsehoods derived from Greek philosophy. In the temple, corruption had become so rampant that Jesus called it "a cave of robbers." (Mark 11:17) Did Jesus stay away from that temple and the synagogues? No! Jehovah was still using those arrangements. Until God stepped in and made changes, Jesus obediently went to the temple festivals and the synagogue.—Luke 4:16; John 5:1.

[20] If Jesus was obedient under those circumstances, how much more so should true Christians remain obedient today! After all, we live in far different times, the long-foretold era of the restoration of pure worship. God assures us that he will never allow Satan to corrupt his restored people. (Isaiah 2:1, 2; 54:17) Granted, we encounter

sins and imperfections within the Christian congregation. But should we use the failings of others as an excuse to disobey Jehovah, perhaps staying away from Christian meetings or becoming critical of the elders? Never! Rather, we heartily support those taking the lead in the congregation. Obediently, we attend Christian meetings and assemblies and apply the Scriptural counsel we receive there.—Hebrews 10:24, 25; 13:17.

[21] Jesus never allowed people, even well-meaning friends, to stop him from obeying Jehovah. The apostle Peter, for instance, tried to persuade his Master that it was not necessary to suffer and die. Jesus firmly rejected Peter's well-intentioned but misguided counsel that Jesus be kind to himself. (Matthew 16:21-23) Today, Jesus' followers often cope with well-meaning relatives who may try to dissuade them from obeying God's laws and principles. Like Jesus' first-century followers, we hold that "we must obey God as ruler rather than men."—Acts 5:29.

Rewards of Christlike Obedience

[22] When Jesus faced death, his obedience was put to the ultimate test. During that dark day, "he learned obedience" in the fullest sense. He did his Father's will, not his own. (Luke 22:42) In the process, he established a perfect record of integrity. (1 Timothy 3:16) He became the answer to the long-standing question: Can a perfect human remain obedient to Jehovah even under test? Adam had failed, and so had Eve. Then Jesus came, lived, died, and set the record straight. The greatest of all of Jehovah's creatures gave the strongest possible answer. He obeyed even when obedience cost him dearly.

---

21. How did Jesus respond to pressure from humans to disobey God, setting what example for us?
22. Jesus gave the answer to what question, and how?

How Can You Follow Jesus?

• What are some of Christ's commands, how may we obey them, and what blessings will result?—John 15:8-19.

• Initially, how did Jesus' relatives feel about his ministry, and what may we learn from the way Jesus handled them?—Mark 3:21, 31-35.

• Why should we never worry that obeying Jehovah might deprive us of a happy life?—Luke 11:27, 28.

• What can we learn from Jesus' willingness to obey a law that did not really apply to him?—Matthew 17:24-27.

²³ Integrity, or wholehearted devotion to Jehovah, is expressed by obedience. Because Jesus obeyed, he preserved his integrity and benefited all mankind. (Romans 5:19) Jehovah richly rewarded Jesus. If we obey our Master, Christ, Jehovah will reward us as well. Obedience to Christ leads to "everlasting salvation"!—Hebrews 5:9.

²⁴ Further, integrity is a reward in itself. Proverbs 10:9 says: "He that is walking in integrity will walk in security." If integrity could be likened to a great mansion made of fine bricks, each act of obedience might be compared to an individual brick. A brick may seem insignificant, but each one has its place, its value. And when many are joined together, something of far greater worth is built up. When obedient acts are brought together, one added to the other, day after day and year after year, we build up the beautiful house of our integrity.

²⁵ A course of obedience that stretches over time brings to mind another quality—endurance. That aspect of Jesus' example is the subject of the next chapter.

23-25. (a) How is obedience related to integrity? Illustrate. (b) What is the subject of the next chapter?

CHAPTER 7

"Consider Closely the One Who Has Endured"

THE pressure is intense. Jesus has never before experienced such mental and emotional anguish. He is in the final hours of his life on earth. Together with his apostles, he comes to a familiar place, the garden of Gethsemane. He has often met with them here. On this night, however, he needs some time alone. Leaving his apostles, he goes deeper into the garden, and kneeling, he begins to pray. He prays so earnestly and gets into such an agony that his sweat becomes "as drops of blood falling to the ground."—Luke 22:39-44.

2 Why is Jesus so troubled? True, he knows that soon he will have to face extreme physical suffering, but that is not the reason for his anguish. Far more important matters weigh on him. He is deeply concerned about his Father's name and recognizes that the future of the human family depends on his remaining faithful. Jesus knows how vital it is that he endure. Were he to fail, he would bring great reproach on Jehovah's name. But Jesus does not fail. Later that day, moments before drawing his last breath, the man who set the finest example of endurance ever on earth cries out triumphantly: "It has been accomplished!"—John 19:30.

3 The Bible urges us to "consider closely the one [Jesus] who has endured." (Hebrews 12:3) Some important questions thus arise: What are some of the trials Jesus en-

---

1-3. (a) How severe is Jesus' agony in the garden of Gethsemane, and what is the cause? (b) What can be said about Jesus' example of endurance, and what questions arise?

dured? What enabled him to endure? How can we follow his example? Before we answer these questions, though, let us examine what endurance involves.

What Is Endurance?

[4] From time to time, all of us are "grieved by various trials." (1 Peter 1:6) Does the fact that we undergo a trial necessarily mean that we are enduring it? No. The Greek noun for "endurance" means "the capacity to hold out or bear up in the face of difficulty." Regarding the kind of endurance referred to by Bible writers, one scholar explains: "It is the spirit which can bear things, not simply with resignation, but with blazing hope . . . It is the quality which keeps a man on his feet with his face to the wind. It is the virtue which can transmute the hardest trial into glory because beyond the pain it sees the goal."

[5] To endure, then, is not simply a matter of experiencing inescapable hardship. In the Biblical sense, endurance involves steadfastness, keeping the right mental attitude and a hopeful outlook in the face of trials. Consider an illustration: Two men are imprisoned in similar conditions but for very different reasons. One, a common criminal, begrudgingly serves his sentence with sad-faced compliance. The other, a true Christian imprisoned for his faithful course, stands his ground and keeps a positive attitude because he sees his situation as an opportunity to demonstrate his faith. The criminal can hardly be considered an example of endurance, whereas the loyal Christian exemplifies this sterling quality.—James 1:2-4.

[6] Endurance is essential if we are to gain salvation.

4, 5. (a) What does "endurance" mean? (b) How might we illustrate that endurance involves more than just experiencing inescapable hardship.
6. How do we cultivate endurance?

(Matthew 24:13) However, we are not born with this vital quality. Endurance must be cultivated. How? "Tribulation produces endurance," says Romans 5:3. Yes, if we truly want to develop endurance, we cannot fearfully withdraw from all tests of faith. Rather, we must face them. Endurance results when day by day we confront and overcome trials large and small. Each test we pass strengthens us to meet the next one. Of course, we do not build endurance on our own. We are "dependent on the strength that God supplies." (1 Peter 4:11) To help us remain steadfast, Jehovah has given us the best possible aid—the example of his Son. Let us take a closer look at Jesus' flawless record of endurance.

What Jesus Endured

7 As the end of his earthly life drew near, Jesus endured cruelty upon cruelty. In addition to the extreme mental stress that he was under on his final night, consider the disappointment he must have felt and the humiliation he suffered. He was betrayed by an intimate associate, abandoned by his closest friends, and subjected to an illegal trial during which members of the highest religious court of the land ridiculed him, spit on him, and hit him with their fists. Yet, he endured it all with quiet dignity and strength.—Matthew 26:46-49, 56, 59-68.

8 In his final hours, Jesus endured tremendous physical suffering. He was scourged, severely beaten in a way that is said to cause "deep stripelike lacerations and appreciable blood loss." He was impaled, executed in a manner that led to "a slow death with maximum pain and suffering." Think about the agony he must have felt as large nails were pounded through his hands and feet,

7, 8. What did Jesus endure as the end of his earthly life drew near?

fastening him to the stake. (John 19:1, 16-18) Imagine the searing pain that seized him as the stake was swung upright and the weight of his body hung from the nails and his torn back scraped against the stake. And he endured this extreme physical suffering while bearing the load described at the outset of this chapter.

⁹ As followers of Christ, what may we have to endure? Jesus said: "If anyone wants to come after me, let him . . . pick up his torture stake and continually follow me." (Matthew 16:24) The expression "torture stake" is here used figuratively to represent suffering, shame, or even death. Following Christ is not an easy course. Our Christian standards make us different. This world hates us because we are no part of it. (John 15:18-20; 1 Peter 4:4) Nevertheless, we are willing to pick up our torture stake —yes, we are prepared to suffer, even die, rather than give up following our Exemplar.—2 Timothy 3:12.

¹⁰ During his ministry, Jesus faced other tests brought on by the imperfections of those around him. Recall that he was the "master worker," whom Jehovah used to create the earth and all life on it. (Proverbs 8:22-31) So Jesus knew what Jehovah purposed for humankind; they were to reflect His qualities and enjoy life in perfect health. (Genesis 1:26-28) When on earth, Jesus saw the tragic results of sin from a different perspective—he himself was a man, able to experience human feelings and emotions. How it must have pained him to see firsthand how far humans had fallen from the original perfection

9. What is involved in picking up our "torture stake" and following Jesus?

10-12. (a) Why did the imperfections of those around him pose a test of endurance for Jesus? (b) What were some of the trialsome situations that Jesus endured?

of Adam and Eve! A test of endurance thus confronted Jesus. Would he get discouraged and give up, viewing sinful humans as a lost cause? Let us see.

¹¹ The unresponsiveness of the Jews caused Jesus such distress that he openly wept. Did he allow their indifference to dampen his zeal or cause him to stop preaching? On the contrary, he "went teaching daily in the temple." (Luke 19:41-44, 47) He was "thoroughly grieved" at the insensibility of the hearts of the Pharisees who were watching closely to see whether he would heal a certain man on the Sabbath. Did he let those self-righteous opposers intimidate him? Certainly not! He stood firm and healed the man—right in the center of the synagogue at that!—Mark 3:1-5.

¹² Something else must have been trialsome for Jesus —the weaknesses of his closest disciples. As we learned

Will we allow opposition to dampen our spirits, or will we continue to preach with zeal?

in Chapter 3, they demonstrated a persistent desire for prominence. (Matthew 20:20-24; Luke 9:46) Jesus counseled them more than once about the need for humility. (Matthew 18:1-6; 20:25-28) Yet, they were slow to respond. Why, on his final night with them, they got into "a heated dispute" about who was the greatest among them! (Luke 22:24) Did Jesus give up on them, reasoning that they were beyond hope? No. Ever patient, he remained positive and hopeful, continuing to see the good in them. He knew that at heart they loved Jehovah and really wanted to do His will.—Luke 22:25-27.

¹³ We may face tests that are similar to those that Jesus endured. For example, we may encounter people who are unresponsive or even opposed to the Kingdom message. Will we allow such negative reactions to dampen our spirits, or will we continue to preach with zeal? (Titus 2:14) We may be tested as a result of the imperfections of our Christian brothers. A thoughtless word or careless deed may hurt our feelings. (Proverbs 12:18) Will we let the shortcomings of fellow believers cause us to give up on them, or will we continue to put up with their faults and look for the good in them?—Colossians 3:13.

Why Jesus Endured

¹⁴ What helped Jesus to stand firm and keep his integrity despite all the indignities, disappointments, and sufferings he faced? There are two outstanding factors that sustained Jesus. First, he looked above, appealing to "the God who supplies endurance." (Romans 15:5) Second, Jesus looked ahead, focusing on what his endurance would lead to. Let us consider these factors one at a time.

---

13. We may face what tests that are similar to those that Jesus endured?
14. What two factors helped Jesus to stand firm?

¹⁵ Jesus, although the perfect Son of God, did not rely on his own strength to endure. Instead, he turned to his heavenly Father and prayed for help from above. The apostle Paul wrote: "Christ offered up supplications and also petitions to the One who was able to save him out of death, with strong outcries and tears." (Hebrews 5:7) Notice that Jesus "offered up" not just petitions but also supplications. The term "supplication" refers to an especially heartfelt and earnest entreaty—yes, a begging for help. The use of the plural "supplications" indicates that Jesus implored Jehovah more than once. Indeed, in the garden of Gethsemane, Jesus prayed repeatedly and fervently.—Matthew 26:36-44.

¹⁶ Jesus had complete confidence that Jehovah would answer his supplications, for he knew that his Father is the "Hearer of prayer." (Psalm 65:2) During his prehuman existence, the firstborn Son had seen how his Father responds to the prayers of loyal worshippers. For example, the Son was an eyewitness in the heavens when Jehovah dispatched an angel to answer the heartfelt prayer of the prophet Daniel—even before Daniel had finished praying. (Daniel 9:20, 21) How, then, could the Father fail to answer when his only-begotten Son poured out his heart "with strong outcries and tears"? Jehovah did respond to the entreaties of his Son and sent an angel to strengthen him to bear up under the ordeal.—Luke 22:43.

¹⁷ To endure, we too must look heavenward—to the God "who imparts power." (Philippians 4:13) If the perfect

---

15, 16. (a) What shows that Jesus did not rely on his own strength to endure? (b) What confidence did Jesus have in his Father, and why?

17. To endure, why should we look heavenward, and how may we do so?

Son of God felt the need to supplicate Jehovah for help, how much more so should we! Like Jesus, we may need to implore Jehovah repeatedly. (Matthew 7:7) Although we do not expect to receive an angelic visit, of this we can be sure: Our loving God will respond to the pleas of the loyal Christian who "persists in supplications and prayers night and day." (1 Timothy 5:5) Regardless of the trials we may face—whether ill health, the death of a loved one, or persecution from opposers—Jehovah will answer our fervent prayers for wisdom, courage, and strength to endure.—2 Corinthians 4:7-11; James 1:5.

[18] The second factor that enabled Jesus to endure is that he looked ahead, beyond the suffering to what lay before him. Of Jesus, the Bible says: "For the joy that was set before him he endured a torture stake." (Hebrews 12:2) Jesus' example illustrates how hope, joy, and endurance work together. This might be summed up as follows: Hope leads to joy, and joy to endurance. (Romans 15:13; Colossians 1:11) Jesus had marvelous prospects. He knew that faithfulness on his part would help to vindicate his Father's sovereignty and enable him to repurchase the human family from

---

18. How did Jesus look beyond his suffering to what lay ahead?

Jehovah will answer our fervent prayers for help to endure

sin and death. Jesus also had the hope of ruling as King and serving as High Priest, to bring further blessings to obedient humans. (Matthew 20:28; Hebrews 7:23-26) By focusing on the prospects and hope before him, Jesus found immeasurable joy, and that joy, in turn, helped him to endure.

[19] Like Jesus, we need to let hope, joy, and endurance work together in our behalf. "Rejoice in the hope," said the apostle Paul. He then added: "Endure under tribulation." (Romans 12:12) Are you facing a severe test of faith at the present time? Then by all means look ahead. Do not lose sight of the way your endurance will bring praise to Jehovah's name. Keep the precious Kingdom hope in clear focus. Picture yourself in God's coming new world, and imagine yourself experiencing the blessings of the Paradise. Anticipating the fulfillment of the wonderful things Jehovah has promised—including the vindication of his sovereignty, the removal of wickedness from the earth, and the elimination of sickness and death—will fill your heart with joy, and that joy can help you to endure no matter what trials may befall you. When compared with the realization of the Kingdom hope, any suffering in this system of things is indeed "momentary and light."—2 Corinthians 4:17.

"Follow His Steps Closely"

[20] Jesus knew that being his follower would be challenging, a course calling for endurance. (John 15:20) He was prepared to lead the way, knowing that his example

---

19. When faced with tests of faith, how can we let hope, joy, and endurance work together in our behalf?
20, 21. When it comes to endurance, what does Jehovah expect of us, and what should be our determination?

How Can You Follow Jesus?

• How might we regard any suffering we may experience because of being a follower of Christ?—Matthew 5:10-12.

• What did Jesus tell his followers to expect, and how can we follow the counsel he gave?—Matthew 10:16-22.

• When facing opposition or persecution, how can we follow Jesus' example?—1 Peter 2:18-25.

• What does faithful endurance under suffering confirm? —1 Peter 4:12-14.

---

would strengthen others. (John 16:33) Granted, Jesus set the perfect example of endurance, but we are far from perfect. What does Jehovah expect of us? Peter explains: "Christ suffered for you, leaving you a model for you to follow his steps closely." (1 Peter 2:21) In the way he dealt with trials, Jesus left "a model," a pattern to be copied.* The record of endurance that he built up may be compared to "steps," or footprints. We cannot follow those steps perfectly, but we can follow them "closely."

21 Let us, then, be determined to follow Jesus' example to the best of our ability. Let us never forget that the more closely we follow in Jesus' footsteps, the better equipped we will be to endure "to the end"—the end of this old system of things or the end of our present life. We do not know which will come first, but we do know this: For all eternity, Jehovah will reward us for our endurance.—Matthew 24:13.

---

* The Greek word translated "model" literally means "underwriting." The apostle Peter is the only writer of the Christian Greek Scriptures to use this word, which is said to mean " 'a copyhead' in a child's exercise book, a perfect piece of writing which the child is to imitate as exactly as it can."

"TEACHING . . . AND PREACHING THE GOOD NEWS"

Carpenter. Miracle worker. Healer.
Jesus was all of these and more. Yet, people
did not use such terms when addressing him.
They called him Teacher. Indeed, his lifework
was "teaching . . . and preaching the good news."
(Matthew 4:23) As followers of Jesus,
we have the same work to do. In this section,
we will study his example, which
shows us the way.

CHAPTER 8

"For This I Was Sent Forth"

THEY have been walking for hours. Jesus and his apostles are trekking northward, heading from Judea toward Galilee. The shortest route—a journey of about three days—takes them through Samaria. As the sun nears its zenith, they approach a small city named Sychar, where they stop for refreshment.

² While his apostles go to buy food, Jesus rests by a well outside the city. A woman approaches to draw water. Jesus could choose to ignore her. He is "tired out from the journey." (John 4:6) It would be understandable if he just closed his eyes and let this Samaritan woman come and go unnoticed. As we saw in Chapter 4 of this book, the woman would likely expect any Jew to treat her with disdain. Yet, Jesus strikes up a conversation with her.

³ He opens with an illustration, one taken from the woman's daily life—indeed, from this very moment. She is here to draw water; Jesus speaks of life-giving water that will quench her spiritual thirst. Several times, she raises points that are potentially controversial.* Jesus

---

* For example, in asking why a Jew addresses a Samaritan, she brings up the subject of the centuries-old feud between the two peoples. (John 4:9) She also asserts that her people descended from Jacob, a claim that the Jews of the day vehemently deny. (John 4:12) They call Samaritans by the name Cuthaeans to emphasize their descent from foreign peoples.

1-4. (a) How does Jesus skillfully teach a Samaritan woman, and with what result? (b) How do his apostles react?

tactfully sidesteps such issues and keeps the conversation on track. He focuses on spiritual matters—pure worship and Jehovah God. His words have far-reaching effects, for the woman relays them to the men of the city, and they too want to listen to Jesus.—John 4: 3-42.

⁴ Upon their return, how do the apostles feel about the remarkable witness that Jesus is giving here? There is no sign of enthusiasm on their part. They are surprised that Jesus is even talking to this woman, and evidently they say nothing to her. After she leaves, they keep urging Jesus to eat the food they have brought. However, Jesus says to them: "I have food to eat of which you do not know." Puzzled, they take his words literally at first. Then he explains: "My food is for me to do the will of him that sent me and to finish his work." (John 4:32, 34) Jesus thus teaches them that his main work in life is more important to him than eating. He wants them to feel the same way about it. What is this work?

⁵ Jesus once said: "I must declare the good news of the kingdom of God, because for this I was sent forth." (Luke 4:43) Yes, Jesus was sent to preach and to teach the good news of God's Kingdom.* Jesus' followers today have the same work to do. It is vital, then, that we consider why Jesus preached, what he preached, and what his attitude toward his assignment was.

_____

* To preach means to proclaim, or declare, a message. To teach is similar in meaning but involves conveying a message in greater depth and detail. Good teaching includes finding ways to reach hearts in order to motivate students to act on what they hear.

_____

5. What was Jesus' lifework, and what will we consider in this chapter?

Why Jesus Preached

⁶ Let us consider how Jesus felt about the truths he taught; then we will discuss his attitude toward the people he taught. Jesus used a vivid illustration to show how he felt about sharing with others the truths Jehovah had taught him. He said: "Every public instructor, when taught respecting the kingdom of the heavens, is like a man, a householder, who brings out of his treasure store things new and old." (Matthew 13:52) Why does the householder in this illustration bring things out of his treasure store?

⁷ The householder is not simply showing off his possessions, the way King Hezekiah of old once did—with painful consequences. (2 Kings 20:13-20) What does motivate the householder? Consider an illustration: You visit a favorite teacher in his home. He opens a desk drawer and pulls out a couple of letters—one of them yellowed with age, the other newer. They are letters that he received from his father—one of them decades ago when the teacher was but a boy, the other in recent times. His eyes gleam with pleasure as he tells you how much he values these letters and how the advice they contain has changed his life and could help you. The letters are clearly treasured by the teacher, holding a cherished place in his heart. (Luke 6:45) He shares them with you, not to boast or to profit in some way, but to benefit you and to convey to you a sense of their worth.

⁸ The Great Teacher, Jesus, had similar motives in sharing God's truths with others. To him, those truths were

---

6, 7. How did Jesus want "every public instructor" to feel about sharing the good news with others? Illustrate.

8. Why do we have good reason to feel that the truths we learn from God's Word are treasures?

treasures beyond price. He loved them, and he was eager to share them. He wanted all his followers, "every public instructor," to feel that way. Do we? We have ample reason to love every truth we learn from God's Word. We treasure gems of truth whether they are long-cherished beliefs or recent refinements. By speaking with heartfelt enthusiasm and maintaining our love for what Jehovah has taught us, we convey that love, as Jesus did.

[9] Jesus also loved the people he taught, as we will discuss more fully in Section 3. Prophecy foretold that the Messiah would "feel sorry for the lowly one and the poor one." (Psalm 72:13) Indeed, Jesus cared about people. He cared about the thoughts and attitudes that drove them; he was concerned about the burdens that weighed them down and the obstacles that hindered them from grasping the truth. (Matthew 11:28; 16:13; 23:13, 15) Recall the Samaritan woman, for example. No doubt she was greatly impressed that Jesus took an interest in her. His insight into her personal situation moved her to accept him as a prophet and to tell others about him. (John 4:16-19, 39) Granted, Jesus' followers today cannot read the hearts of the people to whom they preach. However, we can take an interest in people, as Jesus did; we can let our concern for them show; and we can tailor our words to meet their particular interests, challenges, and needs.

What Jesus Preached

[10] What did Jesus preach? If you were to seek the answer by examining the teachings of many churches that

---

9. (a) How did Jesus feel about the people he taught? (b) How can we imitate Jesus' attitude toward people?
10, 11. (a) What did Jesus preach? (b) How did the need for God's Kingdom arise?

claim to represent him, you might conclude that he proclaimed some kind of social gospel. Or perhaps you would get the impression that he advocated political reform or that he stressed personal salvation above all else. However, as previously noted, Jesus said plainly: "I must declare the good news of the kingdom of God." Just what did that involve?

[11] Remember, Jesus was present in heaven when Satan first challenged the rightness of Jehovah's sovereignty. How it must have pained Jesus to see his righteous Father slandered and accused of being an unjust Ruler who withholds good from His creatures! How hurt God's Son must have been when Adam and Eve, the future parents of humankind, gave heed to Satan's slander! The Son saw that the human family was infected with sin and death as a result of that rebellion. (Romans 5:12) How thrilled he must have been, though, to learn that his Father would one day set matters straight!

[12] Above all else, what needed to be set straight? Jehovah's holy name needed to be sanctified, cleared of every trace of reproach heaped upon it by Satan and all who have sided with him. The rightfulness of Jehovah's sovereignty, his way of ruling, needed to be vindicated. Better than any other man, Jesus understood these vital issues. In the model prayer, he taught his followers to ask first for his Father's name to be sanctified, next for his Father's Kingdom to come, and then for God's will to be done on earth. (Matthew 6:9, 10) God's Kingdom, with Christ Jesus as its Ruler, will soon rid the earth of Satan's corrupt system and confirm Jehovah's righteous rulership for all time.—Daniel 2:44.

12, 13. God's Kingdom will set straight what injustices, and how did Jesus make the Kingdom central to his ministry?

¹³ That Kingdom was the theme of Jesus' ministry. All his words and all his actions helped to clarify what that Kingdom is and how it will serve Jehovah's purpose. Jesus allowed nothing to sidetrack him from his mission to preach the good news of God's Kingdom. In his day, there were pressing social issues, countless injustices, yet his focus was on his message and his work. Did maintaining such a focus mean that Jesus was narrow in his outlook, dull and repetitive in his approach? Far from it!

¹⁴ As we will see throughout this section, Jesus made his teaching both interesting and colorful. He appealed to people's hearts. We might be reminded of wise King Solomon, who sought delightful words, correct words of truth, to convey the thoughts that Jehovah inspired him to write down. (Ecclesiastes 12:10) Jehovah gave that imperfect man "broadness of heart," enabling him to speak about many things, from birds to fish to trees to beasts. People came from far away to hear Solomon speak. (1 Kings 4:29-34) Yet, Jesus was "something more than Solomon." (Matthew 12:42) He was far wiser, with far more "broadness of heart." When teaching people, Jesus drew on his superior knowledge of God's Word as well as of birds, animals, fish, agriculture, weather, current events, history, and social conditions. At the same time, Jesus never showed off his knowledge in order to impress others. He kept his message simple and clear. No wonder people delighted to hear him speak!—Mark 12: 37; Luke 19:48.

¹⁵ Christians today try to follow Jesus' lead. We do not have his immense wisdom and knowledge, but all of us do have a measure of knowledge and experience from

---

14, 15. (a) How did Jesus prove to be "something more than Solomon"? (b) How can we imitate Jesus in what we preach?

which to draw when we share with others the truths of God's Word. Parents, for instance, may draw from their experience in raising children to illustrate Jehovah's love for His children. Others may draw examples or illustrations from secular work, school, or their knowledge of people and current events. At the same time, we are careful not to let anything divert attention from our message —the good news of God's Kingdom.—1 Timothy 4:16.

Jesus' Attitude Toward His Ministry

16 Jesus felt that his ministry was a precious treasure. He delighted in helping people to see his heavenly Father as He truly is, unobscured by confusing man-made doctrines and traditions. Jesus loved helping people gain an approved relationship with Jehovah and the hope of everlasting life. He delighted in bringing people the comfort and joy of the good news. How did he show that he had such feelings? Consider three ways.

17 First, *Jesus made the ministry the primary focus of his life.* Talking about the Kingdom was his career, his lifework, his central interest. That is why, as we noted in Chapter 5, Jesus wisely kept his life simple. As he counseled others, he kept his eye focused on what mattered most. He was not distracted by a lot of things that he would have to pay for, maintain, and repair or replace as time went on. He lived simply so that nothing would needlessly pull him away from his ministry.—Matthew 6:22; 8:20.

18 Second, *Jesus expended himself in his ministry.* He devoted immense energy to it, walking literally hundreds

---

16, 17. (a) What attitude did Jesus have toward his ministry? (b) How did Jesus show that his ministry was the focus of his life?
18. In what ways did Jesus expend himself in his ministry?

of miles throughout Palestine, seeking out people with whom he might share the good news. He spoke to them in their homes, in public squares, in marketplaces, and out in the open. He spoke to them even when he was in need of rest, food, water, or a little quiet time with his closest friends. Even as he was dying, he continued to share with others the good news of God's Kingdom! —Luke 23:39-43.

[19] Third, *Jesus treated the ministry as something urgent.* Remember his conversation with the Samaritan woman at the well outside of Sychar. Jesus' apostles apparently did not see in that situation an urgent need to share the good news with others. Jesus said to them: "Do you not say that there are yet four months before the harvest comes? Look! I say to you: Lift up your eyes and view the fields, that they are white for harvesting."—John 4:35.

[20] Jesus drew that illustration from the season at hand. It was evidently the month of Chislev (November/December). The barley harvest would not come for another four months, about the time of Passover, on Nisan 14. So farmers did not feel any urgency about the harvest just then. It was still a long way off. But what about the harvest of people? Ah, many were ready to hear, to learn, to become Christ's disciples and gain the marvelous hope that Jehovah held out to them. It was as if Jesus could look out over those figurative fields and see that they were white with all the ripe grain swaying gently in the breeze, signaling their readiness to be harvested.* The time was at hand, and the work was urgent!

---

* Regarding this verse, one reference work notes: "Grain, when ripe, turns from a green to a yellow, or light colour, indicating that it is time to reap it."

19, 20. How did Jesus illustrate the urgency of the preaching work?

How Can You Follow Jesus?

● How might our prayers and our actions show that we grasp the urgency of the ministry?—Matthew 9:35-38.

● If we find that our zeal for the ministry is cooling off, how might Jesus' attitude spur us on?—Mark 1:35-39.

● As we preach, how should we view people who are lowly, oppressed, or rejected by others?—Luke 18:35–19:10.

● Why should we never let a mixed or hostile response to our preaching dampen our zeal?—John 7:32-52.

Consequently, when people of one city tried to keep Jesus with them, he replied: "Also to other cities I must declare the good news of the kingdom of God, because for this I was sent forth."—Luke 4:43.

[21] In all three ways just discussed, we can imitate Jesus. We can make the Christian ministry the primary focus of our life. Even though we may have family and secular obligations, we can show that our ministry comes first by having a zealous, regular share in it, as Jesus did. (Matthew 6:33; 1 Timothy 5:8) We can expend ourselves in the ministry, giving generously of our time, energy, and resources to support it. (Luke 13:24) And we can keep ever in mind that our work is urgent. (2 Timothy 4:2) We need to seize every opportunity to preach!

[22] Jesus also showed that he saw the importance of the work by ensuring that it would continue after his death. He commissioned his followers to carry on the preaching and teaching work. That commission will be the subject of the following chapter.

---

21. How can we imitate Jesus?
22. What will be considered in the following chapter?

"Go ... and Make Disciples"

A FARMER faces a real challenge. Some months earlier, he plowed his fields and sowed seeds. He watched with great care as the first blades appeared, and he rejoiced as the plants matured. Now all his hard work is rewarded, for the time to reap has arrived. His dilemma is this: The crop is too abundant for him to gather it alone. To meet this challenge, he wisely decides to hire some workers and send them out into his fields. After all, there is only so much time to gather his precious crop.

2 In the spring of 33 C.E., the resurrected Jesus faces a similar challenge. During his earthly ministry, he sowed

---

1-3. (a) What does a farmer do when the crop is too abundant for him to gather it alone? (b) What challenge does Jesus face in the spring of 33 C.E., and how does he meet it?

What can the farmer do if the crop is too abundant for him to gather it alone?

seeds of truth. Now there is a harvest to reap, and the crop is abundant. Many responsive ones need to be gathered as disciples. (John 4:35-38) How does Jesus meet this challenge? On a mountain in Galilee, shortly before ascending to heaven, he gives his disciples a commission to find more workers, saying: "Go therefore and make disciples of people of all the nations, baptizing them . . . , teaching them to observe all the things I have commanded you."—Matthew 28:19, 20.

³ That commission lies at the very heart of what it means to be a genuine follower of Christ. Let us, then, examine three questions. Why did Jesus issue the commission for more workers? How did he train his disciples to find them? How are we involved in this commission?

Why More Workers Were Needed

⁴ When Jesus began his ministry in 29 C.E., he knew that he was starting a work that he would not finish on his own. In the short time he had left on earth, there was a limit to the area he could cover and the number of people he could reach with the Kingdom message. True, he confined his preaching mainly to Jews and proselytes, "the lost sheep of the house of Israel." (Matthew 15:24) However, those "lost sheep" were scattered throughout the length and breadth of Israel, a land covering thousands of square miles. Besides, the rest of the world field would eventually have to be reached with the good news. —Matthew 13:38; 24:14.

⁵ Jesus recognized that much work would remain to be done after his death. To his 11 faithful apostles, he said: "Most truly I say to you, He that exercises faith in me,

---

4, 5. Why would Jesus not finish the work that he had started, and who would have to carry on the work after he returned to heaven?

that one also will do the works that I do; and he will do works greater than these, because I am going my way to the Father." (John 14:12) Since the Son was returning to heaven, his followers—not just the apostles but also all future disciples—would have to carry on the preaching and teaching work. (John 17:20) Jesus humbly acknowledged that their works would be "greater than" his. How so? In three ways.

6 First, Jesus' followers would *cover more territory.* Today their witnessing has reached the extremities of the earth, far beyond the borders of the land where Jesus himself preached. Second, they would *reach more people.* The small band of disciples Jesus left behind quickly grew into the thousands. (Acts 2:41; 4:4) Now they number into the millions, and hundreds of thousands of new ones are being baptized each year. Third, they would *preach for a longer period of time*—right down to this day, almost 2,000 years after Jesus' ministry of three and a half years ended.

7 Jesus was expressing confidence in his followers when he said that they would do "works greater than these." He was placing in their hands a work that was of utmost importance to him, that of preaching and teaching "the good news of the kingdom of God." (Luke 4:43) He was convinced that they would faithfully carry out the assignment. What does this mean for us today? When we zealously and wholeheartedly pursue the ministry, we show that Jesus' confidence in his followers was not misplaced. Is this not a remarkable privilege?—Luke 13:24.

6, 7. (a) In what ways would the works done by Jesus' followers be greater than his? (b) How can we show that Jesus' confidence in his followers was not misplaced?

Trained to Give a Witness

⁸ Jesus gave his disciples the best possible training for the ministry. Above all, he set a perfect example for them. (Luke 6:40) In the preceding chapter, we discussed his attitude toward the ministry. Consider, for a moment, the disciples who traveled with Jesus on his preaching tours. They observed that he preached wherever people could be found—on lakeshores and hillsides, in cities and marketplaces, and in private homes. (Matthew 5: 1, 2; Luke 5:1-3; 8:1; 19:5, 6) They saw that he was a hard worker, rising early and serving well into the night. The ministry was no casual pastime for him! (Luke 21:37, 38; John 5:17) They no doubt sensed that he was motivated by deep-rooted love for people. Perhaps they saw in his face a reflection of the compassion he felt in his heart. (Mark 6:34) What effect do you think Jesus' example had on his disciples? How would *you* have been affected?

⁹ As followers of Christ, we pattern our ministry after his example. Hence, we leave no stone unturned when it comes to giving "a thorough witness." (Acts 10:42) Like Jesus, we call on people in their homes. (Acts 5:42) We adjust our schedule, if necessary, so that we can call at a time when they are more likely to be at home. We also search out and discreetly preach to people in public places—on streets, in parks, in stores, and in the workplace. We keep "working hard and exerting ourselves" in the ministry, for we take this work seriously. (1 Timothy 4:10) Deep, heartfelt love for others motivates us to keep looking for opportunities to preach wherever and whenever people can be found.—1 Thessalonians 2:8.

8, 9. What example did Jesus set in the ministry, and how can we pattern our ministry after his example?

Love motivates us to preach wherever people can be found

¹⁰ Another way that Jesus trained his disciples was by providing them with extensive instruction. Before sending out first the 12 apostles and later the 70 disciples to preach, Jesus held what amounted to training sessions. (Matthew 10:1-15; Luke 10:1-12) The training produced good results, for Luke 10:17 reports: "The seventy returned with joy." Let us consider two of the important lessons Jesus taught, keeping in mind that his words are to be understood against the background of Jewish customs in Bible times.

¹¹ Jesus taught his disciples *to trust in Jehovah.* He told them: "Do not procure gold or silver or copper for your girdle purses, or a food pouch for the trip, or two undergarments, or sandals or a staff; for the worker deserves his food." (Matthew 10:9, 10) It was common for travelers to take along a girdle purse for money, a food pouch for provisions, and an extra pair of sandals.* By instructing his disciples not to worry about such things, Jesus was, in effect, saying: "Place your trust entirely in Jehovah, for he will take care of your needs." Jehovah would provide for them by moving those who accepted the good news to

---

* A girdle purse was perhaps a type of money belt used to carry coins. A food pouch was a larger bag, usually of leather, slung over the shoulder and used for carrying food or other provisions.

10-12. What important lessons did Jesus teach his disciples before sending them out to preach?

extend hospitality, which was a custom in Israel.—Luke 22:35.

¹² Jesus also taught his disciples to *avoid unnecessary distractions.* He said: "Do not embrace anybody in greeting along the road." (Luke 10:4) Was Jesus telling them to be cool or aloof? Not at all. In Bible times, greetings often involved much more than a simple hello. Customary greetings included various formalities and lengthy conversation. One Bible scholar states: "Salutations among the Orientals did not consist, as among us, of a slight bow, or extension of the hand, but [were] performed by many embraces, and inclinations, and even prostrations of the body on the ground. All this required much *time.*" By telling his disciples not to engage in the customary greetings, Jesus was, in a sense, saying: "You must make the most of your time, for the message you bear is urgent."*

¹³ We take to heart the instructions that Jesus gave his first-century disciples. In carrying out our ministry, we place our complete trust in Jehovah. (Proverbs 3:5, 6) We know that we will never lack the necessities of life if we "keep . . . seeking first the kingdom." (Matthew 6:33) Full-time Kingdom preachers the world over can testify that even during difficult times, Jehovah's hand is never short. (Psalm 37:25) We also recognize the need to avoid distractions. If we are not careful, this system of things

---

* The prophet Elisha once gave similar instructions. When sending his servant Gehazi to the home of a woman whose son had died, Elisha said: "In case you encounter anyone, you must not greet him." (2 Kings 4:29) The mission was urgent, so there was no time for needless delay.

13. In what ways can we demonstrate that we take to heart the instructions that Jesus gave his first-century disciples?

"The seventy returned with joy"

can easily sidetrack us. (Luke 21:34-36) This, however, is no time to be distracted. With lives at stake, our message is urgent. (Romans 10:13-15) Keeping a sense of urgency alive in our hearts will prevent us from allowing the distractions of this world to consume time and energy that would be better spent in the ministry. Remember, the time left is short and the harvest is great.—Matthew 9:37, 38.

A Commission That Involves Us

¹⁴ With the words "Go . . . and make disciples," the resurrected Jesus placed a heavy responsibility upon his followers. He had in mind more than just the disciples who were present that spring day on the mountain in Galilee.* The work he commissioned involves reaching "people of all the nations," and it continues "until the conclusion of the system of things." Clearly, this commission applies to all followers of Christ, including us today. Let us take a closer look at Jesus' words recorded at Matthew 28:18-20.

¹⁵ Before giving the commission, Jesus says: "All authority has been given me in heaven and on the earth." (Verse 18) Does Jesus really have such vast authority? Yes, indeed! He is the archangel, commanding myriads of myriads of angels. (1 Thessalonians 4:16; Revelation 12:7) As "head of the congregation," he has authority

---

* Since most of his followers were in Galilee, it may have been on the occasion described at Matthew 28:16-20 that the resurrected Jesus appeared to "upward of five hundred." (1 Corinthians 15:6) So hundreds may have been present when Jesus gave the commission to make disciples.

---

14. What indicates that the commission recorded at Matthew 28:18-20 applies to all followers of Christ? (See also footnote.)
15. Why are we wise to obey Jesus' command to make disciples?

over his followers on earth. (Ephesians 5:23) Since 1914, he has been ruling as Messianic King in heaven. (Revelation 11:15) His authority reaches even into the grave, for he has the power to resurrect the dead. (John 5:26-28) By first declaring his extensive authority, Jesus indicates that the words that follow are not a suggestion but a command. We are wise to obey, for his authority is not self-assumed but divinely bestowed.—1 Corinthians 15:27.

¹⁶ Jesus now outlines the commission, which begins with a single word: *"Go."* (Verse 19) He thus calls upon us to take the initiative to reach others with the Kingdom message. In fulfilling this aspect of the commission, there is room for a variety of methods. Preaching from house to house is a most effective way to make personal contact with people. (Acts 20:20) We also look for opportunities to witness informally; we are eager to initiate a conversation about the good news wherever appropriate in the course of our daily life. Our specific methods of preaching may vary, being adapted to local needs and circumstances. One thing, though, remains the same: We "go" and search for deserving ones.—Matthew 10:11.

¹⁷ Jesus next explains the objective of the commission, namely, to *"make disciples* of people of all the nations." (Verse 19) How do we "make disciples"? Basically, a disciple is a learner, a taught one. Making disciples, however, is not merely a matter of imparting knowledge to others. When we study the Bible with interested ones, our goal is to help them to become followers of Christ. Whenever possible, we highlight Jesus' example so that our students learn to look to him as their Teacher and Model, living the way he lived and doing the work he did.—John 13:15.

---

16. By telling us to "go," what is Jesus calling upon us to do, and how do we fulfill this aspect of the commission?
17. How do we "make disciples"?

How Can You Follow Jesus?

• In what manner should we approach others with the Kingdom message?—Matthew 10:11-13; Luke 10:5.

• When our preaching work is opposed, how can Jesus' words help us to cope?—Mark 13:9-13.

• How are we to deal with those who are unresponsive to our message?—Luke 10:10, 11.

• When we give priority to the preaching work, what confidence can we have?—Luke 12:22-31.

---

¹⁸ A vital part of the commission is expressed in the words: *"Baptizing* them in the name of the Father and of the Son and of the holy spirit." (Verse 19) Baptism is the most important milestone in a disciple's life, for it is a fitting symbol of his wholehearted dedication to God. Thus, it is essential for salvation. (1 Peter 3:21) Yes, by continuing to do his best in serving Jehovah, the baptized disciple can look forward to endless blessings in the new world to come. Have you helped someone to become a baptized disciple of Christ? In the Christian ministry, there is no greater cause for joy.—3 John 4.

¹⁹ Jesus explains the next part of the commission, saying: *"Teaching* them to observe all the things I have commanded you." (Verse 20) We teach new ones to heed Jesus' commands, including the commands to love God, to love neighbor, and to be disciple makers. (Matthew 22:37-39) We progressively teach them to explain Bible truths and defend their growing faith. When they quali-

---

18. Why is baptism the most important milestone in a disciple's life?
19. What do we teach new ones, and why might the teaching continue after their baptism?

fy to participate in the public preaching activity, we work along with them, teaching them by word and example how to have a meaningful share in this work. The teaching of new disciples is not necessarily finished prior to their baptism. Newly baptized ones may need additional instruction to help them meet the challenges involved in following Christ.—Luke 9:23, 24.

"I Am With You All the Days"

20 The final words of Jesus' commission are most reassuring: "Look! I am with you all the days until the conclusion of the system of things." (Matthew 28:20) Jesus recognizes that this assignment is a weighty one. He also knows that fulfilling it will at times provoke hostile reactions from opposers. (Luke 21:12) There is, however, no reason to fear. Our Leader does not expect us to carry out this assignment unaided or alone. Is it not comforting to know that the One who has "all authority . . . in heaven and on the earth" is with us to support us in fulfilling this commission?

21 Jesus assured his disciples that he would be with them in their ministry throughout the centuries to "the conclusion of the system of things." Until the end comes, we must continue to carry out Jesus' commission. Now is no time to slow down. An abundant spiritual harvest is in progress! Responsive ones are being gathered in great numbers. As followers of Christ, let us be determined to fulfill the weighty commission that has been entrusted to us. Let us be resolved to give of our time, energy, and resources to carry out Christ's command: "Go . . . and make disciples."

20, 21. (a) In carrying out Jesus' commission, why do we have no reason to fear? (b) Why is this no time to slow down, and what should be our determination?

CHAPTER 10

"It Is Written"

IT IS early in Jesus' ministry. Christ has returned to Nazareth, his hometown. His goal is to help the people draw a vital conclusion: He is the long-foretold Messiah! What evidence does he present?

² Many would no doubt expect a miracle. They have heard reports of the amazing works Jesus has performed. He gives them no such sign, however. Rather, he goes to the synagogue, as is his custom. He stands up to read, and the scroll of Isaiah is handed to him. It is a long scroll, likely wound around a pair of rods, and Jesus carefully winds the document from one rod to the other until he finds the passage he seeks. Then he reads aloud what is now Isaiah 61:1-3.—Luke 4:16-19.

³ The audience surely knows the passage. It is a prophecy about the Messiah. Every eye in the synagogue is fixed on Jesus. Silence hangs in the air. Then Jesus begins to explain, perhaps at length: "Today this scripture that you just heard is fulfilled." The audience marvels at his winsome words, but many evidently still want to see some spectacular sign. Instead, Jesus boldly uses a Scriptural example to expose their lack of faith. Soon, the people of Nazareth try to kill him!—Luke 4:20-30.

⁴ Jesus here set a pattern that he maintained throughout

1-3. What vital conclusion does Jesus want the people of Nazareth to draw, and what evidence does he present?

4. Jesus set what pattern in his ministry, and what will we consider in this chapter?

"Today this scripture . . . is fulfilled"

his ministry. He relied heavily on the inspired Word of God. True, his miracles were of great importance in demonstrating that God's spirit was with him. Yet, nothing carried more weight with Jesus than the Holy Scriptures. Let us examine the example he set in this regard. We will consider how our Master quoted from God's Word, defended God's Word, and explained God's Word.

Quoting From God's Word

[5] Jesus wanted people to know where his message came from. He said: "What I teach is not mine, but belongs to him that sent me." (John 7:16) On another occasion, he said: "I do nothing of my own initiative; but just as the Father taught me I speak these things." (John 8:28) Further, he said: "The things I say to you men I do not speak of my own originality; but the Father who remains in union with me is doing his works." (John 14:10) One way that Jesus proved the truth of such comments was by quoting God's written Word again and again.

[6] A close study of Jesus' recorded words reveals that he quoted directly from or referred indirectly to over half of the books of the Hebrew Scripture canon. At first, that may not sound impressive. You may wonder why, in three and a half years of public teaching and preaching, he did not quote from *all* the inspired books available. In truth, though, he may well have done so. Remember, only a fraction of Jesus' words and deeds are recorded. (John 21:25) In fact, you could probably read aloud all of Jesus' recorded words in just a few hours. Now, imagine

---

5. What was Jesus determined to convey to his listeners, and how did he demonstrate the truth of his words?

6, 7. (a) How extensively did Jesus quote from the Hebrew Scriptures, and why is this impressive? (b) How did Jesus' teaching differ from that of the scribes?

talking about God and his Kingdom for just a few hours and managing to work in references to over half of the books of the Hebrew Scriptures! Furthermore, in most cases Jesus did not have written scrolls at hand. When he delivered his famous Sermon on the Mount, he included dozens of direct and indirect references to the Hebrew Scriptures—all from memory!

[7] Jesus' quotations showed his profound reverence for the Word of God. His audience "became astounded at his way of teaching, for there he was teaching them as one having authority, and not as the scribes." (Mark 1: 22) When the scribes taught, they were fond of referring to the so-called oral law, quoting learned rabbis from times past. Jesus never once cited the oral law or some rabbi as an authority. Rather, he viewed God's Word as the final authority. Again and again, we find him saying: "It is written." He repeatedly used those or similar words in teaching his followers and in correcting wrong ideas.

[8] When Jesus cleansed the temple in Jerusalem, he said: "It is written, 'My house will be called a house of prayer,' but you are making it a cave of robbers." (Matthew 21:12, 13; Isaiah 56:7; Jeremiah 7:11) He followed up that courageous act by performing many marvelous works there. Young boys, deeply impressed, began praising him. However, the religious leaders indignantly asked Jesus if he heard what those children were saying. He answered: "Yes. Did you never read this, 'Out of the mouth of babes and sucklings you have furnished praise'?" (Matthew 21:16; Psalm 8:2) Jesus wanted those men to know that God's Word authorized what was happening there.

8, 9. (a) How did Jesus uphold the authority of God's Word when he cleansed the temple? (b) In what way did the religious leaders at the temple show gross disrespect for God's Word?

⁹ Those religious leaders later gathered together and faced Jesus, demanding: "By what authority do you do these things?" (Matthew 21:23) Jesus had made abundantly clear the Source of his authority. He had not innovated, inventing new doctrines. He was simply applying what his Father's inspired Word said. Really, then, those priests and scribes were showing gross disrespect for Jehovah and his Word. They fully merited Jesus' censure as he exposed the wickedness of their motives.—Matthew 21:23-46.

¹⁰ Like Jesus, true Christians today rely on God's Word in the ministry. Jehovah's Witnesses are known the world over for their eagerness to share with others a message from the Bible. Our publications quote and cite the Bible profusely. And in our ministry, we follow suit, endeavoring to feature the Scriptures whenever we talk to people. (2 Timothy 3:16) How it delights us when someone allows us to read from the Bible and to discuss the value and meaning of God's Word! We do not have Jesus' perfect memory, but we do have many tools that were not available to Jesus. In addition to the complete Bible printed in an ever-increasing number of languages, we have many Bible aids to help us find any verse we might seek. Let us be resolved to continue quoting from the Bible and directing people to it at every opportunity!

Defending God's Word

¹¹ Jesus found that God's Word was under frequent attack, but that surely did not surprise him. "Your word is truth," Jesus said to his Father in prayer. (John 17:17) And Jesus well knew that Satan, "the ruler of the world," is "a liar and the father of the lie." (John 8:44; 14:30) In reject-

---

10. How can we imitate Jesus in the way that we use God's Word, and what tools do we have that were not available to Jesus?
11. Why did Jesus frequently have to defend God's Word?

ing Satan's temptations, Jesus quoted from the Scriptures three times. Satan quoted one verse from the Psalms, deliberately misapplying it, and Jesus responded by defending God's Word against this misuse.—Matthew 4:6, 7.

12 Jesus often defended the Holy Scriptures against misuse, misinterpretation, and misrepresentation. The religious teachers of his day represented God's Word in an unbalanced way. They put a lot of emphasis on observing the smallest particulars of the Mosaic Law but very little on applying the principles on which the laws were based. They thus encouraged a superficial form of worship, one concerned with outward appearances rather than with weightier matters—such as justice, mercy, and faithfulness. (Matthew 23:23) How did Jesus defend God's Law?

13 In his Sermon on the Mount, Jesus repeatedly used the phrase "you heard that it was said" to introduce a statute of the Mosaic Law. He would follow up with the phrase "but I say to you" and then expound on a principle that went deeper than the superficial observance of the Law. Was he arguing against the Law? No, he was defending it. For example, the people well knew the law "You must not murder." But Jesus told them that hating a person violated the spirit of that law. Similarly, nourishing passion for a person other than one's mate violated the principle underlying God's law against adultery. —Matthew 5:17, 18, 21, 22, 27-39.

14 Finally, Jesus said: "You heard that it was said, 'You must love your neighbor and hate your enemy.' However, I say to you: Continue to love your enemies and to pray for those persecuting you." (Matthew 5:43, 44) Was the command to "hate your enemy" drawn from

12-14. (a) How did the religious leaders show disrespect for the Mosaic Law? (b) How did Jesus defend God's Word?

God's Word? No, this precept was something that the religious leaders taught of their own originality. They watered down God's perfect Law with human thinking. Jesus fearlessly defended God's Word against the harmful effects of human traditions.—Mark 7:9-13.

15 The religious leaders also attacked God's Law by making it seem unduly strict, even harsh. When Jesus' disciples plucked a few heads of grain while passing through a field, some Pharisees claimed that they were violating the Sabbath. Jesus used a Scriptural example to defend God's Word against this unbalanced view. He cited the only reference in the Scriptures that deals with using the temple showbread outside the sanctuary—when David and his hungry men ate it. Jesus showed those Pharisees that they had missed the point of Jehovah's mercy and compassion.—Mark 2:23-27.

16 Religious leaders also devised legalistic loopholes to weaken the force of God's Law. For instance, the Law allowed a man to divorce his wife if he found "something indecent" on her part, evidently some serious problem that brought shame on the household. (Deuteronomy 24:1) However, by Jesus' day, the religious leaders used that concession as an excuse to allow a man to divorce his wife on all manner of grounds—even for burning his supper!* Jesus showed that they had badly misrepresented Moses' inspired words. He then restored Jehovah's original standard for marriage, that of monogamy, leav-

---

* The first-century historian Josephus, himself a divorced Pharisee, later suggested that divorce was allowable "for any cause whatsoever (and many such causes happen among men)."

---

15. How did Jesus defend God's Law against attempts to make it seem unduly strict, even harsh?
16. What had the religious leaders done to Moses' command regarding divorce, and how did Jesus respond?

ing sexual immorality as the only proper grounds for divorce.—Matthew 19:3-12.

[17] Christ's followers today feel similarly compelled to defend the Sacred Scriptures against attack. When religious leaders imply that the moral standards of God's Word are out-of-date, they are actually attacking the Bible. The Bible is also under attack when religions teach falsehoods and present them as Bible doctrines. We count it a privilege to come to the defense of God's pure Word of truth —showing, for instance, that God is not part of a Trinity. (Deuteronomy 4:39) At the same time, we make any such defense graciously, with genuine mildness and deep respect.—1 Peter 3:15.

Explaining God's Word

[18] Jesus was alive in heaven when the Hebrew Scriptures were recorded. How he must have enjoyed the opportunity to come to the earth and take part in explaining God's Word! Think, for example, of that memorable day after his resurrection when he met up with two of his disciples on the road to Emmaus. Before they recognized who he was, they told him how saddened and confused they were over the death of their beloved Master. How did he respond? "Commencing at Moses and all the Prophets he interpreted to them things pertaining to himself in all the Scriptures." How were they affected? They later said to each other: "Were not our hearts burning as he was speaking to us on the road, as he was fully opening up the Scriptures to us?"—Luke 24:15-32.

[19] Later that same day, Jesus met with his apostles and

---

17. How may Christians today imitate Jesus in defending God's Word?

18, 19. What examples show that Jesus had a marvelous ability to explain God's Word?

others. Note what he did for them: "He opened up their minds fully to grasp the meaning of the Scriptures." (Luke 24:45) No doubt, that happy occasion brought back to their minds the many, many times that Jesus had done something similar for them—and for any who would listen. He often took well-known scriptures and explained them in such a way that something wonderful blossomed in the minds of his listeners—a new and deeper understanding of God's Word.

[20] On one such occasion, Jesus was speaking to a group of Sadducees. They were a sect of Judaism associated with the Jewish priesthood, and they did not believe in the resurrection. Jesus said to them: "As regards the resurrection of the dead, did you not read what was spoken to you by God, saying, 'I am the God of Abraham and the God of Isaac and the God of Jacob'? He is the God, not of the dead, but of the living." (Matthew 22:31, 32) Here was a scripture they knew well, written down by a man that the Sadducees revered—Moses. Do you see, though, the force of Jesus' explanation?

[21] Moses had his conversation with Jehovah at the burning bush about the year 1514 B.C.E. (Exodus 3:2, 6) At that time, Abraham had been dead for 329 years, Isaac for 224, and Jacob for 197. Yet, Jehovah still said: "I *am*" their God. Those Sadducees knew that Jehovah is not like some pagan god of the dead, ruling a mythical underworld. No, he is the God "of the living," as Jesus said. What must that mean? Jesus' conclusion was forceful: "They are all living to him." (Luke 20:38) Jehovah's beloved servants who have died are safely preserved in God's limitless, unfading memory. So sure is Jehovah's purpose to resurrect such ones that they may be spoken of as living. (Romans

---

20, 21. How did Jesus explain the words that Jehovah had spoken to Moses at the burning bush?

How Can You Follow Jesus?

• Why should we be careful never to let human opinion or tradition come ahead of God's Word?—Matthew 15:2-11.

• When we are answering questions, why is it wise to direct attention to the Bible?—Luke 10:25-28.

• How can we imitate Jesus in his willingness to let God's prophetic Word guide his life course and decisions?—Luke 18:31-34; 22:37.

• Whenever our beliefs come under attack, why should we base any defense we make on God's Word?—John 10: 31-39.

4:16, 17) Is that not a marvelous explanation of God's Word? No wonder "the crowds were astounded"!—Matthew 22:33.

²² Christians today have the privilege of imitating Jesus' way of explaining God's Word. Granted, we do not have a perfect mind. Nonetheless, we often get to share with others a scripture they already know and explain to them aspects of it they may never even have considered. For instance, they may have repeated "Hallowed be thy name" and "Thy kingdom come" for a lifetime without ever learning God's name or what his Kingdom is. (Matthew 6:9, 10, *King James Version*) What a wonderful opportunity we have when someone allows us to offer clear, simple explanations of such Bible truths!

²³ Quoting from God's Word, defending it, and explaining it are keys to imitating Jesus' way of sharing the truth. Let us next consider some of the effective methods Jesus used to reach the hearts of his listeners with Bible truths.

22, 23. (a) How may we imitate Jesus in explaining God's Word? (b) What will we consider in the next chapter?

CHAPTER 11

"Never Has Another Man Spoken Like This"

THE Pharisees are filled with anger. Jesus is in the temple, teaching about his Father. Those listening are divided; many put faith in Jesus, while others want him arrested. Unable to contain their anger, the religious leaders dispatch officers to lay hold of Jesus. The officers, however, come back empty-handed. The chief priests and Pharisees demand an explanation: "Why is it you did not bring him in?" The officers reply: "Never has another man spoken like this." They were so impressed with Jesus' teaching that they could not bring themselves to arrest him.* —John 7:45, 46.

2 Those officers were not the only ones impressed with Jesus' teaching. People assembled in great numbers just to hear him teach. (Mark 3:7, 9; 4:1; Luke 5:1-3) Why was Jesus such an outstanding teacher? As we saw in Chapter 8, he loved the truths he conveyed, and he loved the people he taught. He also had a masterful grasp of teaching methods. Let us consider three of the effective methods he used and how we can imitate them.

Keeping It Simple

3 Can you imagine the range of vocabulary that Jesus

---

* The officers were likely agents of the Sanhedrin and under the authority of the chief priests.

1, 2. (a) Why did the officers who were sent to lay hold of Jesus return empty-handed? (b) Why was Jesus an outstanding teacher?
3, 4. (a) Why did Jesus use plain language in his teaching? (b) How is the Sermon on the Mount an example of the simplicity with which Jesus taught?

could have had at his disposal? Yet, when he taught, he never spoke over the heads of his audience, many of whom were "unlettered and ordinary." (Acts 4:13) He was considerate of their limitations, never overwhelming them with too much information. (John 16:12) His words were simple, but the truths they conveyed were nothing less than profound.

4 Take, for example, the Sermon on the Mount, recorded at Matthew 5:3–7:27. Jesus gave counsel in this sermon that goes deep, getting to the very heart of matters. There are no complicated ideas or phrases. Why, there is hardly a word that even a young child cannot readily grasp! No wonder, then, that when Jesus finished, the crowds —likely including many farmers, shepherds, and fishermen—"were astounded at his way of teaching."—Matthew 7:28.

5 In his teaching, Jesus often used simple, short phrases and uttered sayings that were rich in meaning. In an era long before printed books, he thus implanted his message indelibly in the minds and hearts of his listeners. Consider some examples: "Stop judging that you may not be judged." "Persons in health do not need a physician, but the ailing do." "The spirit . . . is eager, but the flesh is weak." "Pay back Caesar's things to Caesar, but God's things to God." "There is more happiness in giving than there is in receiving."* (Matthew 7:1; 9:12; 26:41; Mark 12:17; Acts 20:35) Nearly 2,000 years after they were first spoken, those sayings are as memorable as ever.

* This last statement, found at Acts 20:35, is quoted only by the apostle Paul. He may have received it by word of mouth (either from someone who heard Jesus say it or from the resurrected Jesus) or by divine revelation.

5. Give examples of sayings uttered by Jesus that were simple but rich in meaning.

⁶ How can we teach with simplicity? One important requirement is that we use plain language that most people can readily grasp. The basic truths of God's Word are not complicated. Jehovah has revealed his purposes to those who have sincere and humble hearts. (1 Corinthians 1: 26-28) Simple words carefully chosen can effectively convey the truths of God's Word.

⁷ To teach with simplicity, we must be careful to avoid overwhelming a Bible student with too much information. Thus, when conducting a Bible study, we do not need to explain every detail; nor is it necessary to rush through the material as if covering a set amount of pages is of primary importance. Rather, it is wise to let the student's needs and abilities determine the pace of the study. Our goal is to help the student to become a follower of Christ and a worshipper of Jehovah. To that end, we need to take whatever time is necessary for the student to get a reasonable grasp of what he is learning. Only then will

---

6, 7. (a) To teach with simplicity, why is it important that we use plain language? (b) How can we avoid overwhelming a Bible student with too much information?

When you teach, keep it simple

Bible truth touch his heart and move him to apply what he has learned.—Romans 12:2.

Asking the Right Questions

8 Jesus made remarkable use of questions, even when it would have taken less time just to tell his listener the point. Why, then, did he ask questions? At times, he used penetrating questions to expose the motives of his opposers, thereby silencing them. (Matthew 21:23-27; 22:41-46) In many cases, however, he used questions to get his disciples to express what was on their minds and to stimulate and train their thinking. Hence, he asked such questions as, "What do you think?" and "Do you believe this?" (Matthew 18:12; John 11:26) With his questions, Jesus reached and touched the hearts of his disciples. Consider an example.

9 On one occasion, tax collectors asked Peter if Jesus paid the temple tax.* Peter immediately answered, "Yes." Later, Jesus reasoned with him: "What do you think, Simon? From whom do the kings of the earth receive duties or head tax? From their sons or from the strangers?" Peter responded: "From the strangers." Jesus said: "Really, then, the sons are tax-free." (Matthew 17:24-27) The point of the questions was no doubt obvious to Peter, for the family members of kings were known to be tax-exempt. Therefore, as the only-begotten Son of the heavenly King

---

* The Jews were required to pay an annual temple tax of two drachmas, which was about two days' wages. One reference work says: "This tax was chiefly utilized to defray the expenses of the daily burnt-offering and of all the sacrifices in general made in the name of the people."

8, 9. (a) Why did Jesus ask questions? (b) How did Jesus use questions to help Peter reach the right conclusion on the matter of paying the temple tax?

who was worshipped at the temple, Jesus was not under obligation to pay the tax. Note that rather than just telling Peter the right answer, Jesus tactfully used questions to help Peter reach the right conclusion and perhaps see the need to think more carefully before answering in the future.

Ask questions that are tailored to the interests of the householder

¹⁰ How can we make effective use of questions in our ministry? When preaching from house to house, we can use questions to arouse interest, perhaps opening the way for us to share the good news. For example, if an older person comes to the door, we might respectfully bring up the question, "How has the world changed in your lifetime?" After allowing for a response, we might then ask, "What do you think it would take to make this world a better place in which to live?" (Matthew 6:9, 10) If a mother with small children answers the door, we could ask, "Have you ever wondered what this world will be like when your children grow up?" (Psalm 37:10, 11) By being observant when we approach a house, we may be able to choose a question that is tailored to the interests of the householder.

¹¹ How can we put questions to good use when conducting a Bible study? Carefully chosen questions can help us to draw out the feelings of the student's heart. (Proverbs 20:5) For example, suppose we are studying the chapter

10. How can we make effective use of questions when preaching from house to house?
11. How can we put questions to good use when conducting a Bible study?

"Living in a Way That Pleases God" in the book *What Does the Bible Really Teach?** The chapter discusses God's view of such matters as sexual immorality, drunkenness, and lying. The student's answers may indicate that he understands *what* the Bible teaches, but does he *agree* with what he is learning? We might ask, "Does God's view of such matters seem reasonable to you?" We might also ask, "How can you apply this information in your life?" Keep in mind, though, the need to be tactful, according the student dignity. We never want to ask questions that needlessly embarrass him.—Proverbs 12:18.

Employing Powerful Logic

¹² With his perfect mind, Jesus was a master at reasoning with others. At times, he employed powerful logic to refute the false charges of his opposers. In many instances, he used persuasive reasoning to teach his followers valuable lessons. Let us look at some examples.

¹³ After Jesus healed a demon-possessed man who was blind and unable to speak, the Pharisees charged: "This fellow does not expel the demons except by means of Beelzebub [Satan], the ruler of the demons." They conceded that superhuman power was needed to expel the demons. However, they attributed Jesus' power to Satan. The charge was not only false but also illogical. Exposing the error of their thinking, Jesus replied: "Every kingdom divided against itself comes to desolation, and every city or house divided against itself will not stand. In the same way, if Satan expels Satan, he has become divided against himself; how, then, will his kingdom stand?"

---

* Published by Jehovah's Witnesses.

12-14. (a) In what ways did Jesus use his ability to employ logical reasoning? (b) What powerful logic did Jesus use when the Pharisees attributed his power to Satan?

(Matthew 12:22-26) Jesus was, in effect, saying: "If I were an agent of Satan, undoing what Satan did, then Satan would be working against his own interests and would soon fall." How could they refute such convincing logic?

¹⁴ Jesus had not yet finished reasoning with them. Knowing that some of the Pharisees' own disciples had cast out demons, he asked a simple but powerful question: "If I expel the demons by means of Beelzebub, by means of whom do your sons [or, disciples] expel them?" (Matthew 12:27) Jesus' argument, in a sense, was this: "If I expel demons by means of the power of Satan, then your own disciples must be using this same power." What could the Pharisees say? They would never acknowledge that their disciples acted under Satan's power. Jesus thus pressed their faulty reasoning to what was for them a very uncomfortable conclusion. Is it not thrilling just to read about how Jesus reasoned with them? Imagine, though, the crowds who heard Jesus firsthand, for his presence and the tone of his voice no doubt increased the force of his words.

¹⁵ Jesus also used logical, persuasive reasoning to teach positive, heartwarming truths about his Father. He often did so by employing a "how much more so" line of reasoning—helping his listeners to advance from a familiar truth to an even stronger conviction.* Based on contrast, this type of reasoning can make a deep impression. Let us examine just two examples.

¹⁶ When responding to his disciples' request to teach

---

* This type of reasoning is sometimes termed "a fortiori," a Latin expression meaning "for a still stronger reason; even more certain; all the more."

15-17. Relate an example of how Jesus used a "how much more so" line of reasoning to teach heartwarming truths about his Father.

them how to pray, Jesus described the willingness of imperfect human parents "to give good gifts" to their children. He then concluded: "If you, although being wicked, know how to give good gifts to your children, *how much more so* will the Father in heaven give holy spirit to those asking him!" (Luke 11:1-13) The point Jesus made is based on contrast. If sinful human parents care for the needs of their children, how much more will our heavenly Father, who is perfect and righteous in every way, grant holy spirit to his loyal worshippers who humbly approach him in prayer!

[17] Jesus used similar reasoning when offering wise counsel on dealing with anxiety. He said: "The ravens neither sow seed nor reap, and they have neither barn nor storehouse, and yet God feeds them. Of *how much more* worth are you than birds? Mark well how the lilies grow; they neither toil nor spin . . . If, now, God thus clothes the vegetation in the field that today exists and tomorrow is cast into an oven, *how much rather* will he clothe you, you with little faith!" (Luke 12:24, 27, 28) If Jehovah cares for birds and flowers, how much more will he care for humans who love and worship him! With such reasoning, Jesus no doubt touched the hearts of his listeners.

[18] In our ministry, we want to use sound logic to refute false beliefs. We also want to use persuasive reasoning to teach positive truths about Jehovah. (Acts 19:8; 28:23, 24) Must we learn to employ sophisticated logic? Not at all. The lesson we learn from Jesus is that logical arguments presented in a simple manner are most effective.

[19] For instance, how might we respond if someone says that he does not believe in a God he cannot see? We could

18, 19. How might we reason with someone who says that he does not believe in a God he cannot see?

reason on the natural law of cause and effect. When we observe an effect, we realize that there must be a cause. We might say: "If you were in a remote area and came across a well-built house that was stocked with food (effect), would you not readily acknowledge that someone (a cause) was responsible? So, too, when we see the obvious design built into nature and the abundance of food stocked in earth's 'cupboards' (effect), does it not make sense to conclude that Someone (a Cause) is responsible? The Bible itself reasons in this way: 'Every house is constructed by someone, but he that constructed all things is God.'" (Hebrews 3:4) Of course, no matter how sound our reasoning, not everyone will be convinced.—2 Thessalonians 3:2.

20 In our teaching, whether in the field ministry or in

20, 21. (a) How can we use a "how much more so" line of reasoning to highlight Jehovah's qualities and ways? (b) What will we discuss in the next chapter?

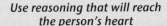

*Use reasoning that will reach
the person's heart*

How Can You Follow Jesus?

• How might Jesus' comments help you to choose your words when you are giving talks in the congregation?—Matthew 11:25.

• In what ways can public speakers imitate Jesus' use of this type of question?—Matthew 11:7-9.

• How might you make discreet use of hyperbole in your teaching?—Matthew 7:3; 19:24.

• How could we, like Jesus, use object lessons in teaching others?—John 13:5, 14.

the congregation, we can also use the "how much more so" line of reasoning to highlight Jehovah's qualities and ways. For example, to show that the doctrine of eternal torment in hellfire actually dishonors Jehovah, we might say: "What loving father would punish his child by holding his child's hand in a fire? How much more must the very idea of hellfire be repugnant to our loving heavenly Father!" (Jeremiah 7:31) To assure a depressed fellow believer of Jehovah's love for him, we could say: "If Jehovah considers even a tiny sparrow to be of value, how much more must he care about and love each of his earthly worshippers, including you!" (Matthew 10:29-31) Such reasoning can help us to reach the hearts of others.

21 After examining just three of the teaching methods that Jesus used, we can easily see that those officers who failed to arrest him were not overstating matters when they said: "Never has another man spoken like this." In the next chapter, we will discuss the teaching method for which Jesus is perhaps best known, that of using illustrations.

CHAPTER 12

"Without an Illustration He Would Not Speak to Them"

THE disciples traveling with Jesus have a rare privilege. They are learning directly from the Great Teacher. They get to hear his voice as he opens up the meaning of God's Word and teaches them thrilling truths. For now, they must carry his precious sayings in their minds and hearts; it is not yet the time for his words to be preserved in writing.* However, Jesus makes it easier for them to remember what he teaches. How? By his way of teaching, especially his masterful use of illustrations.

2 Indeed, effective illustrations are not quickly forgotten. One author noted that illustrations "turn ears into eyes" and that they "free listeners to think with pictures in their heads." Because we often think best in pictures, illustrations can make even abstract ideas easier to grasp. Illustrations can bring words to life, teaching us lessons that become etched in our memory.

3 No teacher on earth has ever been more skillful at using illustrations than was Jesus Christ. To this day, his illustrations are easily recalled. Why did Jesus rely heavily on this method of teaching? What made his illustrations so effective? How can we learn to use this teaching method?

---

* The first inspired record of Jesus' earthly life was evidently the Gospel of Matthew, written about eight years after Jesus' death.

1-3. (a) The disciples traveling with Jesus have what rare privilege, and how does he make it easier for them to remember what he teaches? (b) Why are effective illustrations easy to remember?

Why Jesus Taught With Illustrations

⁴ The Bible gives two important reasons why Jesus used illustrations. First, his doing so fulfilled prophecy. At Matthew 13:34, 35, we read: "Jesus spoke to the crowds by illustrations. Indeed, without an illustration he would not speak to them; that there might be fulfilled what was spoken through the prophet who said: 'I will open my mouth with illustrations.'" The prophet mentioned by Matthew was the writer of Psalm 78:2. That psalmist wrote under the inspiration of God's spirit centuries before Jesus' birth. Consider what this means. Hundreds of years in advance, Jehovah determined that the Messiah would teach with illustrations. Surely, then, Jehovah must value this method of teaching.

⁵ Second, Jesus explained that he used illustrations to sift out those whose hearts had "grown unreceptive." (Matthew 13:10-15; Isaiah 6:9, 10) What was it about his illustrations that exposed the motives of people? In some cases, he wanted his listeners to ask for an explanation in order to get the full meaning of his words. Humble individuals were willing to ask, whereas haughty or indifferent ones were not. (Matthew 13:36; Mark 4:34) Jesus' illustrations, then, *revealed* truth to those whose hearts hungered for it; at the same time, his illustrations *concealed* truth from those with proud hearts.

⁶ Jesus' illustrations served a number of other beneficial purposes. They aroused interest, compelling people to listen. They painted mental images that were easy to grasp. As noted at the outset, Jesus' illustrations helped his listeners to remember his words. The Sermon on the Mount, as recorded at Matthew 5:3–7:27,

---

4, 5. Why did Jesus use illustrations?
6. Jesus' illustrations served what beneficial purposes?

is an outstanding example of Jesus' generous use of word pictures. According to one count, this sermon contains over 50 figures of speech. To put that in perspective, keep in mind that this sermon can be read aloud in about 20 minutes. At that rate, a figure of speech is uttered, on average, nearly every 20 seconds! Clearly, Jesus saw the value of painting a picture with words!

7 As followers of Christ, we want to imitate his way of teaching, including his use of illustrations. Like the seasonings that make a meal more appetizing, effective illustrations can make our teaching more appealing to others. Well-thought-out word pictures can also make important truths easier to grasp. Let us now take a closer look at some of the factors that made Jesus' illustrations so effective. Then we will be able to see how we can put this valuable teaching method to good use.

Using Simple Comparisons

8 In his teaching, Jesus often used comparisons that were uncomplicated, requiring just a few words. Yet, the simple words painted vivid mental images and clearly taught important spiritual truths. For example, when urging his disciples not to be anxious over daily needs, he pointed to "the birds of heaven" and "the lilies of the field." The birds do not sow and reap, nor do the lilies spin and weave. Still, God cares for them. The point is easy to see —namely, that if God takes care of birds and flowers, surely he will look after humans who "keep . . . seeking first the kingdom."—Matthew 6:26, 28-33.

9 Jesus also made generous use of metaphors, which are even more forceful comparisons. A metaphor refers to

7. Why imitate Jesus' use of illustrations?
8, 9. How did Jesus make use of simple comparisons, and what made the comparisons he drew so effective?

one thing as if it *were* another. Here, again, he kept the comparisons simple. On one occasion, he told his disciples: "You are the light of the world." The disciples could hardly miss the point of the metaphor, namely, that through their words and deeds, they could let the light of spiritual truth shine and help others to give glory to God. (Matthew 5:14-16) Note some other metaphors used by Jesus: "You are the salt of the earth" and "I am the vine, you are the branches." (Matthew 5:13; John 15:5) Such figures of speech are powerful in their simplicity.

[10] How can you use illustrations in your teaching? You do not have to come up with long, elaborate stories. Just try to think of simple comparisons. Imagine that you are discussing the subject of the resurrection and that you want to illustrate that raising the dead poses no problem for Jehovah. What comparison comes to mind? The Bible uses sleep as a metaphor for death. You might say, "God can resurrect the dead as easily as we can awaken someone from sleep." (John 11:11-14) Suppose that you want to illustrate that children need love and affection if they are to thrive. What example could you use? The Bible uses this comparison: Children are "like slips [new shoots] of olive trees." (Psalm 128:3) You could say, "Love and affection are to a child what sunshine and water are to a tree." The simpler the comparison, the easier it will be for your listeners to get the point.

Drawing From Everyday Life

[11] Jesus was a master at using illustrations that related to the lives of people. Many of his illustrations reflected

---

10. What are some examples that show how you can use illustrations in your teaching?
11. Give examples of how Jesus' illustrations reflected things that he had no doubt observed while growing up in Galilee.

everyday circumstances that he had likely observed while growing up in Galilee. Think, for a moment, about his early life. How often did he see his mother grind grain into flour, add leaven to dough, light a lamp, or sweep the house? (Matthew 13:33; 24:41; Luke 15:8) How many times did he watch the fishermen as they let down their nets into the Sea of Galilee? (Matthew 13:47) How often did he observe children playing in the marketplace? (Matthew 11:16) Jesus no doubt saw other commonplace things that are mentioned in his many illustrations—seeds being sown, joyful wedding feasts, and grain fields ripening in the sun.—Matthew 13:3-8; 25:1-12; Mark 4:26-29.

¹² In his illustrations, Jesus mentioned details that were well-known to his listeners. For example, he began the parable of the neighborly Samaritan by saying: "A certain man was going down from Jerusalem to Jericho and fell among robbers, who both stripped him and inflicted blows, . . . leaving him half-dead." (Luke 10:30) Significantly, Jesus referred to the road that went "from Jerusalem to Jericho" to make his point. When relating this parable, he was in Judea, not far from Jerusalem; so his listeners undoubtedly knew about the road in question. That road was known to be dangerous, especially for someone traveling alone. It wound through lonely terrain, providing many lurking places for robbers.

¹³ Jesus included other familiar details about the road that went "from Jerusalem to Jericho." According to the parable, first a priest and then a Levite were also traveling that road—although neither stopped to help the victim. (Luke 10:31, 32) The priests served at the temple in Jerusalem, and the Levites assisted them. Many priests and

12, 13. Why is it significant that Jesus used the road that went "from Jerusalem to Jericho" to make his point in the parable of the neighborly Samaritan?

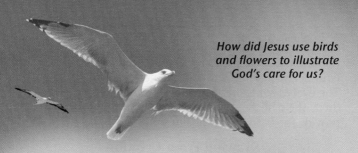

How did Jesus use birds and flowers to illustrate God's care for us?

Levites resided in Jericho when they were not working at the temple; Jericho was only 14 miles from Jerusalem. Hence, they could be seen on that road. Note, too, that Jesus spoke of the traveler as "going down"—not up—the road "from Jerusalem." This made sense to his listeners. Jerusalem was higher in elevation than Jericho. Therefore, when traveling "from Jerusalem," a traveler would indeed be "going down."* Jesus clearly kept his listeners in mind.

¹⁴ When we use illustrations, we too need to keep our audience in mind. What are some things about our listeners that might have a bearing on our choice of illustrations? Perhaps such factors as age, cultural or family background, and

---

* Jesus also said that the priest and the Levite were coming *"from* Jerusalem," thus going away from the temple. Thus, no one could excuse their indifference by saying that they avoided the man who appeared to be dead because they did not want to become temporarily unfit to serve at the temple.—Leviticus 21:1; Numbers 19:16.

---

14. When using illustrations, how can we keep our audience in mind?

occupation come into play. For instance, an illustration that mentions details about farming might be more readily understood in an agricultural area than in a large city. The everyday life and activities of our hearers—their children, their house, their hobbies, their food—might also provide the basis for fitting illustrations.

Drawing From Creation

15 Many of Jesus' illustrations reveal his knowledge of the natural world, including plants, animals, and the elements. (Matthew 16:2, 3; Luke 12:24, 27) Where did he get such knowledge? While growing up in Galilee, he no doubt had ample opportunity to observe creation. More significantly, Jesus is "the firstborn of all creation," and in creating all things, Jehovah used him as the "master worker." (Colossians 1:15, 16; Proverbs 8:30, 31) Is it any wonder that Jesus was intimately acquainted with creation? Let us see how he put this knowledge to skillful use.

16 Recall that Jesus identified himself as "the fine shepherd" and his followers as "the sheep." Jesus' words indicate that he was very familiar with the traits of domestic sheep. He knew that there was a unique bond between shepherds and their sheep. He noted that these trusting creatures readily allowed themselves to be led and that they faithfully followed their shepherd. Why do sheep follow their shepherd? "Because they know his voice," said Jesus. (John 10:2-4, 11) Do sheep really know their shepherd's voice?

17 From personal observation, George A. Smith wrote in his book *The Historical Geography of the Holy Land:*

---

15. Why is it no wonder that Jesus was intimately acquainted with creation?
16, 17. (a) What indicates that Jesus was very familiar with the traits of sheep? (b) What example shows that sheep really do listen to the voice of their shepherd?

"Sometimes we enjoyed our noonday rest beside one of those Judaean wells, to which three or four shepherds come down with their flocks. The flocks mixed with each other, and we wondered how each shepherd would get his own again. But after the watering and the playing were over, the shepherds one by one went up different sides of the valley, and each called out his peculiar call; and the sheep of each drew out of the crowd to their own shepherd, and the flocks passed away as orderly as they came." Jesus could hardly have found a better illustration to make his point, namely, that if we recognize and obey his teachings and if we follow his lead, then we can come under the care of "the fine shepherd."

[18] How can we learn to use illustrations that are drawn from creation? The outstanding traits of animals may provide the basis for simple but effective comparisons. Where can we find information about Jehovah's creations? The

18. Where can we find information about Jehovah's creations?

Bible is a rich source of knowledge about a variety of animals, and at times, it uses animal traits in an illustrative way. The Bible alludes to being as swift as a gazelle or a leopard, as cautious as a snake, and as innocent as a dove.* (1 Chronicles 12:8; Habakkuk 1:8; Matthew 10:16) Other valuable sources of information are *The Watchtower, Awake!,* and other literature produced by Jehovah's Witnesses. You can learn much from observing how these publications employ simple comparisons drawn from the wonders of Jehovah's many creations.

Drawing From Familiar Examples

[19] Effective illustrations can take the form of real-life examples. On one occasion, Jesus used a recent event to expose as false the belief that tragedy befalls those who deserve it. He said: "Those eighteen upon whom the tower in Siloam fell, thereby killing them, do you imagine that they were proved greater debtors [sinners] than all other men inhabiting Jerusalem?" (Luke 13:4) Indeed, those 18 souls did not perish because of some sin that provoked divine displeasure. Rather, their tragic death was a result of "time and unforeseen occurrence." (Ecclesiastes 9:11) Jesus thus refuted a false teaching by referring to an event that was well-known to his hearers.

[20] How can we use true-life examples and experiences in our teaching? Suppose that you are discussing the fulfillment of Jesus' prophecy concerning the sign of his presence. (Matthew 24:3-14) You might refer to recent news

---

* For a more comprehensive list of the Bible's figurative use of animal traits, see *Insight on the Scriptures,* Volume 1, pages 268, 270-1, published by Jehovah's Witnesses.

19, 20. (a) To expose a false belief, how did Jesus make effective use of a recent event? (b) How can we use true-life examples and experiences in our teaching?

How Can You Follow Jesus?

● What aspects of creation did Jesus use in his illustrations, and how might you use similar examples?—Matthew 13:24-32.

● How did Jesus use a simple illustration to make a powerful point, and what do you learn from his example?—Matthew 18:12-14.

● What everyday experiences did Jesus draw on, and how might his example help you to choose illustrations?—Luke 11: 5-8; 12:6.

---

items about wars, famines, or earthquakes to show that specific features of the sign are being fulfilled. Or imagine that you want to use an experience to illustrate the changes involved in putting on the new personality. (Ephesians 4:20-24) Where can you find such an experience? You could consider the varied backgrounds of fellow believers, or you might use an experience printed in one of the publications of Jehovah's Witnesses.

²¹ Truly, Jesus was the Master Teacher! As we have seen in this section, "teaching . . . and preaching the good news" was his lifework. (Matthew 4:23) It is our lifework too. The rewards of being an effective teacher are great. When we teach, we are giving to others, and such giving brings happiness. (Acts 20:35) That happiness is the joy of knowing that we are imparting something of genuine and lasting value—the truth about Jehovah. We can also have the satisfaction that comes from knowing that we are following the example of Jesus, the greatest Teacher ever to walk the earth.

---

21. What rewards come from being an effective teacher of God's Word?

"THE LOVE THE CHRIST HAS COMPELS US"

What motivates us to keep following Jesus? The apostle Paul answers: "The love the Christ has compels us." (2 Corinthians 5:14) In this section we will study the love that Jesus has—for Jehovah, for mankind, and for us as individuals. Such a study is truly compelling. Our hearts are touched, and we feel compelled to act, to make progress in following our Master's example.

CHAPTER 13

"I Love the Father"

AN AGED man dips his pen in ink, his mind full of memories. His name is John, and he is the last living apostle of Jesus Christ. Now about 100 years old, John casts his thoughts back some seven decades to a most memorable evening—the last one that he and his fellow apostles spent with Jesus before His death. With God's holy spirit guiding him, John is able to remember and write down events in great detail.

² That night, Jesus made it clear that he would soon be put to death. John alone reveals the reason *why* Jesus said that he was going to submit to that terrible end: "In order for the world to know that I love the Father, even as the Father has given me commandment to do, so I am doing. Get up, let us go from here."—John 14:31.

³ "I love the Father." Nothing mattered more to Jesus than that. Not that he constantly repeated the statement. In fact, John 14:31 is the only place in the Bible record where we find Jesus expressing his love for his Father so directly. Yet, Jesus *lived* those words. His love for Jehovah was in evidence daily. Jesus' courage, his obedience, and his endurance were all evidence of his love for God. His entire ministry was motivated by this love.

⁴ Today, some may think of love as a soft quality. They

1, 2. What did the apostle John reveal about the final evening that the apostles spent with Jesus?

3. How did Jesus show that he loved his Father?

4, 5. The Bible promotes what kind of love, and what can be said about Jesus' love for Jehovah?

may think of love poems and love songs, perhaps even of the giddiness that is sometimes associated with romantic love. The Bible does discuss romantic love, although in a more dignified way than is common now. (Proverbs 5:15-21) God's Word spends much more time, though, on discussing love of another kind. This love is not mere passion or fleeting emotion; nor is it a dry, intellectual philosophy. It involves both heart and mind. Such love springs from the innermost self, is governed by and in harmony with noble principles, and is expressed in positive action. It is anything but frivolous. "Love never fails," says God's Word.—1 Corinthians 13:8.

⁵ Of all humans who have ever lived, Jesus was the foremost lover of Jehovah. No one has surpassed Jesus in living by the words he himself quoted as the greatest of all divine commands: "You must love Jehovah your God with your whole heart and with your whole soul and with your whole mind and with your whole strength." (Mark 12:30) How did Jesus develop such love? How did he keep his love for God strong during his time on earth? And how can we imitate him?

The Oldest and Strongest Bond of Love

⁶ Have you ever worked on a project with a friend and found that the two of you became better, closer friends as a result? That pleasant experience may provide some insight into the love that developed between Jehovah and his only-begotten Son. We have referred more than once to Proverbs 8:30, but let us take a closer look at that verse in its context. In verses 22 through 31, we find an inspired description of wisdom personified. How do we know that these words refer to God's Son?

6, 7. How do we know that Proverbs 8:22-31 describes God's Son, not just the quality of wisdom?

[7] In verse 22, wisdom says: "Jehovah himself produced me as the beginning of his way, the earliest of his achievements of long ago." More than just wisdom must be involved here, for that quality never was "produced." It never began to exist because Jehovah has always existed and he has always been wise. (Psalm 90:2) God's Son, however, was "the firstborn of all creation." He was produced, or created; he was the earliest of all of Jehovah's achievements. (Colossians 1:15) The Son existed before the earth and the heavens, as described in Proverbs. And as the Word, God's own Spokesman, he was the perfect expression of Jehovah's wisdom.—John 1:1.

[8] How was the Son occupied during the vast expanse of time before he came to earth? Verse 30 tells us that he was beside God as "a master worker." What does that mean? Colossians 1:16 explains: "By means of him all other things were created in the heavens and upon the earth . . . All other things have been created through him and for him." So Jehovah, the Creator, worked through his Son, the Master Worker, to bring every other creation into existence—from the spirit creatures in the heavenly realm to the immense physical universe, to the earth with its wondrous variety of plant and animal life, to the pinnacle of earthly creation: humankind. In some respects, we might liken this cooperation between Father and Son to that of an architect working with a builder, or contractor, who specializes in bringing the architect's ingenious designs to reality. When we are awed by any facet of creation, we are actually giving credit to the Great Architect. (Psalm 19:1) However, we may also call to mind the long and happy collaboration between the Creator and his "master worker."

---

8. How was the Son occupied during his prehuman existence, and what might we think about when admiring creation?

⁹ When two imperfect humans work closely together, they sometimes have a difficult time getting along. Not so with Jehovah and his Son! The Son worked for aeons with the Father and was "glad before him *all* the time." (Proverbs 8:30) Yes, he delighted in his Father's company, and the feeling was mutual. Naturally, the Son grew ever more like his Father, learning to imitate God's qualities. No wonder, then, that the bond between Father and Son became so strong! It can rightly be called the oldest and strongest bond of love in the whole universe.

¹⁰ What, though, can that mean for us? You might feel that you could never build such a bond with Jehovah. Granted, none of us has the exalted position of the Son. However, we do have a remarkable opportunity. Remember, Jesus drew closer to his Father by working with Him. Jehovah lovingly offers us the opportunity to be his "fellow workers." (1 Corinthians 3:9) As we follow Jesus' example in the ministry, we should always keep in mind that we are God's fellow workers. Thus, the bond of love that unites us with Jehovah grows ever stronger. Could there be any greater privilege?

How Jesus Kept His Love for Jehovah Strong

¹¹ In many ways, it is helpful to think of the love in our heart as a living thing. Like a beautiful houseplant, love needs to be nourished and cared for if it is to grow and to thrive. Neglected, deprived of nourishment, it weakens and dies. Jesus did not take his love for Jehovah for grant-

---

9, 10. (a) What strengthened the bond between Jehovah and his Son? (b) What can strengthen your bond with your heavenly Father?
11-13. (a) Why is it helpful to think of love as a living thing, and how did young Jesus keep his love for Jehovah strong? (b) How did God's Son show his interest in learning from Jehovah, both before coming to earth and later as a man?

ed. He kept it strong and thriving throughout his earthly sojourn. Let us see how.

12 Think again of the incident when young Jesus spoke up at the temple in Jerusalem. Recall his words to his anxious parents: "Why did you have to go looking for me? Did you not know that I must be in the house of my Father?" (Luke 2:49) As a young boy, Jesus evidently did not yet have any memory of his prehuman existence. Still, his love for his Father, Jehovah, was intense. He knew that such love naturally found its expression in worship. So there was no place on earth as appealing to Jesus as his Father's house of pure worship. He longed to be there and hated to leave. Moreover, he was no passive spectator. He was eager to learn about Jehovah and to express what he knew. Such feelings did not begin when he was 12 years old, nor did they end at that age.

13 In his prehuman existence, the Son had eagerly learned from his Father. A prophecy recorded at Isaiah 50:4-6 reveals that Jehovah gave his Son specialized education regarding his role as the Messiah. Even though such education included learning about some of the hardships that would befall Jehovah's Anointed One, the Son learned eagerly. Later, after Jesus came to earth and grew to adulthood, he remained eager to go to his Father's house and share in the worship and the learning that Jehovah wanted to see promoted there. The Bible thus reports on Jesus' faithful attendance at the temple and at the synagogue. (Luke 4:16; 19:47) If we want to keep our love for Jehovah alive and thriving, we need to be diligent about attending Christian meetings, where we worship Jehovah and deepen our knowledge and appreciation of him.

¹⁴ Jesus also kept his love for Jehovah strong by praying regularly. Although he was a friendly, gregarious man, it is striking to note that he valued solitude. For example, Luke 5:16 says: "He continued in retirement in the deserts and praying." Similarly, Matthew 14:23 states: "Eventually, having sent the crowds away, he went up into the mountain by himself to pray. Though it became late, he was there alone." Jesus sought solitude on these and other occasions, not because he was a recluse or hated the company of others, but because he wanted to be alone with Jehovah, to speak freely with his Father in prayer.

¹⁵ When he prayed, Jesus would at times use the expression *"Abba,* Father." (Mark 14:36) In Jesus' day, "Abba" was an intimate word for "father," a family word. It was often among the first words that a child would learn. Yet, it was respectful. While the word revealed the intimacy of the Son speaking to his beloved Father, it also conveyed profound respect for Jehovah's fatherly authority. We find that combination of intimacy and respect throughout Jesus' recorded prayers. For example, in John chapter 17, the apostle John recorded the long and heartfelt prayer that Jesus offered on His final night. It is truly moving for us to study that prayer and vital that we imitate it—not by repeating Jesus' words, of course, but by finding ways to speak from the heart to our heavenly Father as often as we can. Doing so will keep our love for him alive and strong.

¹⁶ As we noted earlier, Jesus did not repeatedly utter the words "I love the Father." However, many times he did

---

14, 15. (a) Why did Jesus seek solitude? (b) How did Jesus' prayers to his Father reveal intimacy and respect?

16, 17. (a) How did Jesus put his love for his Father into words? (b) How did Jesus portray his Father's generosity?

"He went up into the mountain by himself to pray"

put his love for his Father into words. How so? Jesus himself said: "I *publicly praise* you, Father, Lord of heaven and earth." (Matthew 11:25) When studying Section 2 of this book, we saw that Jesus loved to praise his Father by helping people get to know Him. For example, he likened Jehovah to a father who was so eager to forgive his wayward son that he awaited the repentant young man's arrival, caught sight of him from afar, and ran to meet him and embrace him. (Luke 15:20) Who can read that passage without feeling warmed by Jesus' portrayal of Jehovah's love and forgiveness?

[17] Jesus often praised his Father for His generosity. He used the example of imperfect parents to show how certain we can be that our Father will give us all the holy spirit we need. (Luke 11:13) Jesus also spoke about the hope that the Father so generously offers. Jesus longingly described his own hope of being restored to a place by his Father's side in heaven. (John 14:28; 17:5) He told his followers about the hope that Jehovah held out to Christ's "little flock"—that of residing in heaven and sharing in the rule of the Messianic King. (Luke 12:32; John 14:2) And he consoled a dying wrongdoer with the hope of life in Paradise. (Luke 23:43) Speaking of his Father's great generosity in these ways surely helped Jesus to keep his love for Jehovah strong. Many of Christ's followers have found that nothing strengthens their love for Jehovah or their faith in him more than speaking about him and the hope he provides for those who love him.

Will You Imitate Jesus' Love for Jehovah?

[18] Of all the ways in which we need to follow Jesus, none is more important than this: We must love Jehovah with

18. What is the most important way in which we need to follow Jesus, and why?

our whole heart, soul, mind, and strength. (Luke 10:27) The measure of such love is not just in the intensity of our feelings but also in the reality of our actions. Jesus was not content merely to *feel* love for his Father nor merely to *say*, "I love the Father." He said: "In order for the world to know that I love the Father, even as the Father has given me commandment to do, *so I am doing.*" (John 14:31) Satan had charged that no human would serve Jehovah out of unselfish love. (Job 2:4, 5) In order to give the best possible answer to Satan's vicious slander, Jesus courageously went ahead and showed the world just how much he loved his Father. He obeyed even to the point of giving up his life. Will you follow Jesus? Will you show the world that you truly love Jehovah God?

[19] We have a profound spiritual need to show such love. Jehovah has thus arranged for us to worship in a way that our love for our Father is nourished and strengthened. When you attend Christian meetings, try to remember that you are there to worship your God. Facets of that worship include joining in heartfelt prayer, singing songs of praise, listening attentively, and participating when possible. Such meetings also give you an opportunity to encourage fellow Christians. (Hebrews 10:24, 25) Worshipping Jehovah regularly at Christian meetings will help you to grow ever stronger in your love for God.

[20] Much the same can be said for doing personal study, meditating, and praying. Think of these as ways to be alone with Jehovah. As you study God's written Word and meditate on it, Jehovah is conveying his thoughts to

---

19, 20. (a) For what important reasons do we want to be regular in attendance at Christian meetings? (b) How might we view our personal study, meditation, and prayer?

How Can You Follow Jesus?

• When we pray, how can we show confidence in Jehovah, as Jesus did?—John 11:41, 42; Hebrews 11:6.

• How can we express heartfelt love for Jehovah in the way we use his name?—John 17:6-8.

• Why does love for Jehovah require that we imitate Jesus in remaining separate from the world?—John 17:14-16; James 4:8.

• How can we apply Jesus' counsel about maintaining intense love for Jehovah?—Revelation 2:1-5.

---

you. As you pray, you are opening your heart to him. Remember that prayer involves more than just asking God for things. Prayer is also an opportunity to thank Jehovah for the blessings you have received and to praise him for his marvelous works. (Psalm 146:1) Additionally, praising Jehovah publicly with joy and enthusiasm is the best way to thank Jehovah and to show that you love him.

[21] Love for God is the key to your eternal happiness. It is all that Adam and Eve would have needed in order to succeed—and the one thing that they failed to develop. It is the most important thing that you need in order to pass any test of faith, reject any temptation, endure any trial. It is at the very heart of being a follower of Jesus. Of course, love for God is connected to love for our fellow man. (1 John 4:20) In the ensuing chapters, we will examine how Jesus showed his love for people. In the next chapter, we will consider why so many found Jesus approachable.

---

21. How important is love for Jehovah, and what will be considered in the ensuing chapters?

CHAPTER 14

"Great Crowds Approached Him"

JESUS knows that the end of his earthly life is fast approaching. He has just a few weeks left, and there is still so much to do! He is preaching with his apostles in Perea, a region east of the Jordan River. They are working their way south toward Jerusalem, where Jesus will attend his final, climactic Passover.

2 After Jesus has a weighty discussion with some religious leaders, there is a small disturbance. People are bringing their children to see him. Evidently, the children vary in age, for Mark refers to them by the same word that he earlier used to describe a child of 12, while Luke uses a word that can be rendered "infants." (Luke 18:15; Mark 5:41, 42; 10:13) Of course, wherever there are children, there is often some exuberant noise and commotion. Jesus' disciples reprimand the parents, perhaps assuming that the Master is too busy to bother with the children. What does Jesus do?

3 When he sees what is going on, Jesus is indignant. With whom? The children? The parents? No—with his disciples! He says: "Let the young children come to me; do not try to stop them, for the kingdom of God belongs to suchlike ones. Truly I say to you, Whoever does not receive the kingdom of God like a young child will by no means enter into it." Then Jesus takes the children "into his arms," blessing them. (Mark 10:13-16) Mark's language here suggests that Jesus affectionately embraces

1-3. What happens when parents bring their children to Jesus, and what does this incident reveal about Jesus?

them, perhaps even cradling some infants "in the crook of his arm," as one translator puts it. Clearly, Jesus is fond of children. However, we learn something else about him here—he is approachable.

⁴ If Jesus had been a stern, cold, or proud man, likely those children would not have been drawn to him; nor would their parents have felt free to approach him. As you picture the scene, can you not just see the parents beaming as this kind man shows his affection for their children, acknowledges the children's worth in God's eyes, and blesses them? Indeed, though Jesus was burdened with the heaviest of responsibilities, he remained the most approachable of men.

⁵ Who else found Jesus approachable? What made him so easy to approach? And how can we learn to be like Jesus in this regard? Let us see.

Who Found Jesus Approachable?

⁶ As you read the Gospel accounts, you may be struck by the way that great numbers of people did not hesitate to approach Jesus. For example, in connection with him, we often read of "great crowds." "Great crowds followed him from Galilee." "Great crowds gathered to him." "Great crowds approached him." "Great crowds were traveling with him." (Matthew 4:25; 13:2; 15:30; Luke 14:25) Yes, Jesus was often surrounded by multitudes of people.

⁷ Generally, these were the common folk, those whom the religious leaders contemptuously referred to as "people of the land." The Pharisees and priests openly said:

4, 5. (a) How can we be sure that Jesus was approachable? (b) What questions will we examine in this chapter?

6-8. Jesus was often in the company of whom, and how did his attitude toward them differ from that of the religious leaders?

"This crowd that does not know the Law are accursed people." (John 7:49) Later rabbinic writings confirm that attitude. Many religious leaders viewed such people as contemptible, refusing to eat with them, buy from them, or associate with them. Why, some insisted that there was no hope of a resurrection for such ones who did not know the oral law! Many lowly people must have shied away from such leaders rather than asking them for help or guidance. But Jesus was different.

8 Jesus mingled freely with the common people. He ate with them, healed them, taught them, and gave them hope. Of course, Jesus was realistic, acknowledging that most would reject the opportunity to serve Jehovah. (Matthew 7:13, 14) However, he viewed each individual with hope and saw in many the potential to do what was right. What a contrast to those hard-hearted priests and Pharisees! Surprisingly, though, even priests and Pharisees approached Jesus, and a number of them did change their ways and follow him. (Acts 6:7; 15:5) Some of the rich and powerful also found Jesus to be approachable. —Mark 10:17, 22.

9 Women did not hesitate to approach Jesus. They must often have felt the withering contempt of religious leaders. The rabbis generally frowned upon teaching women. In fact, women were not allowed to testify in legal cases; they were viewed as unreliable witnesses. The rabbis even said a prayer in which they thanked God that they were not women! Yet, women found no such contempt in Jesus. Many approached him, eager to learn. For instance, we find Lazarus' sister Mary sitting at the Lord's feet, absorbed in listening to Jesus'

9. Why did women find Jesus approachable?

words while her sister, Martha, bustled about and fretted over the preparation of food. Jesus commended Mary for setting proper priorities.—Luke 10:39-42.

[10] The sick too flocked to Jesus, although they were often treated as outcasts by the religious leaders. The Mosaic Law had provisions for quarantining lepers for health reasons, but there was no basis for unkindness. (Leviticus, chapter 13) Later rabbinic rules, however, stated that lepers were as offensive as excrement. Some religious leaders went so far as to throw stones at lepers to keep them at a distance! It is hard to imagine how those who had been treated that way could summon the courage to approach any teacher, but lepers did approach Jesus. One uttered this famous expression of faith: "Lord, if you just want to, you can make me clean." (Luke 5:12) In the next chapter, we will discuss Jesus' response. For now, suffice it to say that there could hardly be more vivid proof that Jesus was approachable.

[11] Those who felt burdened by guilt freely approached Jesus. Think, for example, of the time when Jesus was dining at the home of a Pharisee. A woman who was known to be a sinner came in and knelt at Jesus' feet, weeping over her guilt. Her tears bathed his feet, and she used her hair to dry them. While Jesus' host recoiled and judged Jesus harshly for allowing this woman to come near, Jesus kindly commended the woman for her sincere repentance and assured her of Jehovah's forgiveness. (Luke 7:36-50) Today more than ever, people who

---

10. How was Jesus different from the religious leaders in the way he dealt with the sick?

11. What example shows that those burdened with guilt felt free to approach Jesus, and why is this important?

"Let the young children come to me"

are loaded down with guilt need to feel free to approach those who can help them make things right with God! What was it that made Jesus so approachable?

What Made Jesus Approachable?

[12] Remember that Jesus perfectly imitated his beloved heavenly Father. (John 14:9) The Bible reminds us that Jehovah "is not far off from each one of us." (Acts 17:27) The "Hearer of prayer," Jehovah, is ever accessible to his faithful servants and to any others who sincerely want to find him and serve him. (Psalm 65:2) Just imagine—the most powerful and important Personage in the universe is also the most approachable! Like his Father, Jesus loves people. In the chapters that follow, we will discuss the love that ran deep in Jesus' heart. Jesus was approachable, though, largely because his love for people was easy to see. Let us examine some of Jesus' traits that demonstrated such love.

[13] People readily sensed that *Jesus was personally interested in them.* That personal interest did not vanish when Jesus was under pressure. As we have already seen, when those parents brought their children to him, Jesus remained approachable even when he was busy, loaded down with weighty responsibilities. What an example he set for parents! Raising children is a challenge in today's world. Yet, it is vital that children see their parents as approachable. If you are a parent, you know that there are times when you are too busy to give your child the attention he calls for. Still, can you assure him that you will make time for him as soon as possible? As you keep your word, your child will learn the rewards of patience. He

12. Why is it not surprising that Jesus was approachable?
13. How might parents imitate Jesus?

will also learn that he is always welcome to approach you with any problem or care.

[14] Jesus conveyed to people that *their concerns mattered to him.* For instance, consider the first miracle Jesus performed. He was attending a wedding feast in Cana, a town in Galilee. An embarrassing problem arose—the wine ran out! Jesus' mother, Mary, told her son what had happened. And what did Jesus do? He had the attendants fill up six large stone jars with water. When a sample was taken to the director of the feast, why, it was fine wine! Was that a trick, some sleight of hand? No, the water "had been turned into wine." (John 2:1-11) Turning one thing into another has long been a dream of humans. For centuries, men called alchemists tried to turn lead into gold. They never succeeded—although lead and gold are, in fact, remarkably similar elements.* What about water and wine? Chemically, water is simple, a combination of two basic elements. Wine, on the other hand, contains nearly a thousand components, many of them complex compounds! Why would Jesus perform such a marvelous deed in answer to something as trivial as a shortage of wine at a wedding feast?

[15] The problem was not trivial to the bride and groom. In the ancient Middle East, hospitality to invited guests was of profound importance. Running out of wine at the wedding feast would have caused the bride and groom

---

* Students of chemistry know that lead and gold are quite close on the periodic table of elements. An atom of lead simply has three more protons in its nucleus than gold has. Modern-day physicists have even converted small amounts of lead into gold, but the process requires so much energy that it is not cost-effective.

14-16. (a) What circumstances led Jesus to perform his first miracle, and why was it a marvelous deed? (b) What does Jesus' miracle in Cana reveal about him, providing what lesson for parents?

Show your child that you are approachable and that you really care

considerable shame and embarrassment, casting a pall over their wedding day and their memories of it in the years that followed. The problem mattered to them, and it mattered to Jesus. So he did something about it. Can you see why people would approach him with their concerns?

16 Again, parents may find a useful lesson here. What if your child approaches you, weighed down with some problem? You may be tempted to dismiss his concern as something trivial. You may even be tempted to laugh about it. Compared to your own burdens, the child's problem may indeed seem insignificant. Remember, though, that it is not trivial to the child! If it matters to one you love so dearly, should it not matter to you as well? Conveying to your child that you care about his concerns will make you an approachable parent.

¹⁷ As we discussed in Chapter 3, *Jesus was mild and humble.* (Matthew 11:29) Mildness is a beautiful quality, powerful proof of the humility in a person's heart. It is part of the fruitage of God's holy spirit and is associated with godly wisdom. (Galatians 5:22, 23; James 3:13) Even under the worst provocation, Jesus maintained control of himself. His mildness was anything but weakness. One scholar said of this quality: "Behind the gentleness there is the strength of steel." Indeed, it often takes strength for us to restrain our temper and treat others with mildness. But with Jehovah blessing our efforts, we can imitate Jesus in showing mildness, and that will make us more approachable.

¹⁸ *Jesus was reasonable.* When Jesus was in Tyre, a woman came to him because her daughter was "badly demonized." In three different ways, Jesus indicated that he was not inclined to do what she wanted. First, he responded with silence; second, he gave her a reason why he should not do as she asked; third, he gave an illustration that made the point even clearer. Yet, was his manner cold, unyielding? Did he imply that she was on dangerous ground in daring to counter the words of so great a man? No, this woman clearly felt safe. She not only asked for help but persisted even in the face of his apparent unwillingness to help her. Jesus saw the remarkable faith that moved her to persist, and he healed her daughter. (Matthew 15:22-28) Surely Jesus' reasonableness, his willingness to listen and to yield when appropriate, made people eager to approach him!

---

17. Jesus set what example of mildness, and why is this quality an evidence of strength?
18. What example reveals Jesus' reasonableness, and why do you think this quality would make a person approachable?

Are You Approachable?

[19] People like to think of themselves as being approachable. Some in positions of authority, for instance, are fond of saying that they have an open-door policy, that their subordinates are always free to approach them. The Bible, however, contains this powerful caution: "A multitude of men will proclaim each one his own loving-kindness, but a faithful man who can find?" (Proverbs 20:6) It is easy to say that we are approachable, but are we truly faithful in imitating this aspect of Jesus' love? The answer may lie, not in how we see ourselves, but in how others see us. Paul said: "Let your reasonableness become known to all men." (Philippians 4:5) Each of us does well to ask: 'How am I perceived by others? What is my reputation?'

[20] Christian elders in particular strive to be approachable. They earnestly desire to live up to the description recorded at Isaiah 32:1, 2: "Each one must prove to be like a hiding place from the wind and a place of concealment from the rainstorm, like streams of water in a waterless country, like the shadow of a heavy crag in an exhausted land." An elder can provide

Elders strive to be approachable

---

19. How can we tell if we are truly approachable?
20. (a) Why is it important for Christian elders to be approachable? (b) Why should we be reasonable in what we expect of elders in the congregation?

How Can You Follow Jesus?

• Why might our asking questions and listening carefully to answers move people to approach us?—Matthew 16:13-17.

• How did Jesus prove to be approachable even when his privacy was interrupted, and how might we follow his example? —Mark 6:31-34.

• How did Jesus view nonbelievers, and how will imitating his balanced view make us approachable?—Luke 5:29-32.

• In what way will imitating Jesus' positive view of people help us to become more approachable?—John 1:47.

such protection, refreshment, and relief only if he remains approachable. Granted, doing so is not always easy, for elders bear a heavy load of responsibility in these difficult times. Still, elders strive never to appear too busy to care for the needs of Jehovah's sheep. (1 Peter 5:2) Other members of the congregation try to be reasonable in what they expect of such faithful men, showing a humble and cooperative spirit.—Hebrews 13:17.

21 Parents seek to be ever available to their children. So much is at stake! They want their children to know that it is safe to confide in Father or Mother. Thus, Christian parents are careful to be mild and reasonable, not overreacting when a child confesses to a mistake or displays some faulty thinking. As parents patiently train their children, they strive to keep the lines of communication open. Really, all of us want to remain approachable, as Jesus was. In the next chapter, we will discuss Jesus' heartfelt compassion—one of the principal qualities that made him approachable.

---

21. How can parents remain accessible to their children, and what will we consider in the next chapter?

CHAPTER 15

"Moved With Pity"

TWO blind men are sitting beside the road, just outside Jericho. They come there each day, find a place where crowds are likely to pass, and publicly ask for charity. This day, however, they are about to experience something that will dramatically change their life.

[2] Suddenly, the beggars hear a commotion. Unable to see what is going on, one of them asks what the excitement is about, and he is told: "Jesus the Nazarene is passing by!" Jesus is on his way to Jerusalem for the last time. But he is not alone; large crowds are following him. Upon hearing who is passing by, the beggars cause something of an uproar by shouting: "Lord, have mercy on us, Son of David!" Annoyed, the crowds tell the beggars to be quiet, but the men are desperate. They will not be silenced.

[3] Jesus hears their shouting above the din of the crowd. What will he do? There is much weighing on his mind and heart. He is about to enter the final week of his earthly life. He knows that suffering and a cruel death await him at Jerusalem. Still, he does not ignore the insistent cries. He stops and asks that the ones doing the shouting be brought to him. "Lord, let our eyes be opened," they plead. "Moved with pity," Jesus touches their eyes, and

1-3. (a) How does Jesus respond when two blind beggars plead with him for help? (b) What is meant by the expression "moved with pity"? (See footnote.)

"Lord, let our eyes be opened"

they recover sight.* Without delay, they begin to follow
Jesus.—Luke 18:35-43; Matthew 20:29-34.

⁴ This was no isolated case. On many occasions and
under many different circumstances, Jesus was deeply
moved to show compassion. Bible prophecy foretold that
he would "feel sorry for the lowly one." (Psalm 72:13)
True to those words, Jesus was sensitive to the feelings of
others. He took the initiative to help people. His compassion was a motivating force in his preaching. Let us see
how the Gospels reveal the tender compassion behind
Jesus' words and actions and consider how we can show
similar compassion.

Consideration for the Feelings of Others

⁵ Jesus was a man of deep empathy. He identified with
and shared in the feelings of those who were suffering.
Even though he did not share all their circumstances, he
truly felt their pain in his heart. (Hebrews 4:15) When
healing a woman who had suffered from a flow of blood
for 12 years, he described her ailment as a "grievous sickness," thus acknowledging that it had caused her great
distress and suffering. (Mark 5:25-34) When he saw Mary
and those with her weeping over the death of Lazarus,
he was so deeply touched by their sorrow that he became inwardly agitated. Although he knew that he was

---

* The Greek word rendered "moved with pity" has been called one
of the strongest words in Greek for the feeling of compassion. One
reference work notes that this word indicates "not only a pained feeling at [the] sight of suffering, but in addition a strong desire to re-
lieve and to remove the suffering."

---

4. How did Jesus fulfill the prophecy that he would "feel sorry for
the lowly one"?

5, 6. What examples show that Jesus was a man of empathy?

about to resurrect Lazarus, Jesus was so moved that his eyes brimmed with tears.—John 11:33, 35.

⁶ On another occasion, a leper approached Jesus and pleaded: "If you just want to, you can make me clean." How did Jesus, a perfect man who had never been sick, respond? His heart went out to the leper. Indeed, "he was moved with pity." (Mark 1:40-42) He then did something extraordinary. He well knew that lepers were unclean under the Law and were not to mingle with others. (Leviticus 13:45, 46) Jesus was certainly capable of healing this man without any physical contact. (Matthew 8:5-13) Yet, he chose to reach out and touch the leper, saying: "I want to. Be made clean." Immediately the leprosy vanished. What tender empathy Jesus expressed!

⁷ As Christians, we are called on to imitate Jesus in showing empathy. The Bible urges us to show "fellow feeling."* (1 Peter 3:8) It may not be easy to grasp the feelings of those suffering from chronic illness or depression—especially if we have not gone through such pain ourselves. Remember, though, that empathy does not depend on shared circumstances. Jesus empathized with the sick even though he himself had never been sick. How, then, can we cultivate empathy? By patiently listening as suffering ones open up their hearts and share their feelings. We might ask ourselves, 'If I were in their situation, how would I feel?' (1 Corinthians 12:26) If we sharpen our sensitivity to the feelings of others, we will be better able to "speak consolingly to the depressed souls." (1 Thessalonians 5:14) At times, empathy may be

---

* The Greek adjective rendered "fellow feeling" literally means "suffering with."

7. What can help us to cultivate empathy, and how may this quality be expressed?

expressed not only with words but also with tears. "Weep with people who weep," says Romans 12:15.

Show "fellow feeling"

[8] Jesus was considerate of others, and he acted in ways that spared their feelings. Recall the time when a man who was deaf and hardly able to speak was brought to Jesus. Evidently sensing some uneasiness in this man, Jesus did something that he did not ordinarily do when healing others: "He took [the man] away from the crowd." In private and free from the stares of the crowd, he healed the man.—Mark 7:31-35.

[9] Jesus acted with similar consideration when people brought him a blind man and asked that he be healed. Jesus "took the blind man by the hand" and "brought him outside the village." He then healed the man in stages. This perhaps allowed the man's brain and eyes to adjust gradually to the dazzling sights and complexities of the sunlit world around him. (Mark 8:22-26) What consideration Jesus showed!

[10] Being followers of Jesus calls on us to show consideration for the feelings of others. We are thus mindful of our speech, remembering that thoughtless use of the tongue can hurt the feelings of others. (Proverbs 12:18; 18:21) Harsh words, disparaging remarks, and biting sarcasm have no place among Christians, who are sensitive to the feelings of other people. (Ephesians 4:31) El-

8, 9. How did Jesus show consideration for the feelings of others?
10. In what ways can we show consideration for the feelings of others?

ders, how can you show consideration for the feelings of others? When giving counsel, cushion your words with kindness, allowing the listener to keep his dignity. (Galatians 6:1) Parents, how can you be considerate of your children's feelings? When administering discipline, endeavor to do so in ways that spare your children needless embarrassment.—Colossians 3:21.

Taking the Initiative to Help Others

[11] Jesus did not always have to be asked before he showed compassion to others. After all, compassion is, not a passive quality, but an active, positive one. Not surprisingly, then, tender compassion moved Jesus to take the initiative in helping others. For example, when a large crowd stayed with him for three days, going without food, no one had to tell Jesus that the people were hungry or suggest that he do something about it. The account says: "Jesus called his disciples to him and said: 'I feel pity for the crowd, because it is already three days that they have stayed with me and they have nothing to eat; and I do not want to send them away fasting. They may possibly give out on the road.'" Then, entirely of his own volition, he fed the crowd miraculously.—Matthew 15:32-38.

[12] Consider another account. In 31 C.E., as Jesus neared the city of Nain, he came across a sad scene. A funeral procession was leaving the city, perhaps heading for nearby hillside tombs, to bury "the only-begotten son of . . . a widow." Can you imagine the pain in that mother's heart? She was about to bury her only son, and she had no husband to share her grief. Of all the people in the procession, Jesus "caught sight of" the now childless

---

11, 12. What Bible accounts show that Jesus did not have to be asked before he displayed compassion to others?

widow. What he saw touched him—yes, "he was moved with pity for her." No one had to implore him. The compassion in his heart impelled him to take the initiative. So "he approached and touched the bier," and then he restored the young man to life. What happened next? Jesus did not ask the young man to join the large crowd traveling with Him. Instead, Jesus "gave him to his mother," making them a family again and ensuring that the widow would be cared for.—Luke 7:11-15.

[13] How can we follow Jesus' example? Of course, we cannot provide food miraculously or restore the dead to life. We can, however, imitate Jesus in taking the initiative to help those in need. A fellow believer may suffer a severe financial reversal or lose his job. (1 John 3:17) The home of a widow may be in urgent need of repair. (James 1:27) We may know of a bereaved family that needs comfort or some practical aid. (1 Thessalonians 5:11) In cases of genuine need, we do not have to wait to be asked before offering some help. (Proverbs 3:27) Compassion will move us to take appropriate initiative to assist, as our circumstances allow. Never forget that a simple act of kindness or a few words of comfort spoken from the heart can be powerful expressions of compassion.—Colossians 3:12.

Compassion Moved Him to Preach

[14] As we saw in Section 2 of this book, Jesus set an outstanding example in preaching the good news. He said: "I must declare the good news of the kingdom of God, because for this I was sent forth." (Luke 4:43) Why did he give priority to this work? Primarily because of his love

---

13. How can we imitate Jesus in taking the appropriate initiative to help those in need?
14. Why did Jesus give priority to the work of preaching the good news?

Take the initiative to help those in need

for God. But Jesus had another motive: Heartfelt compassion moved him to respond to the spiritual needs of others. Of all the ways that he showed compassion, none were more important than satisfying the spiritual hunger of others. Let us examine two incidents that reveal how Jesus viewed the people to whom he preached. Such a consideration can help us to analyze our own motives for sharing in the public ministry.

¹⁵ In 31 C.E., after about two years of exerting himself vigorously in the ministry, Jesus expanded his efforts by embarking "on a tour of all the cities and villages" of Galilee. What he saw touched his heart. The apostle Matthew reports: "On seeing the crowds he felt pity for them, because they were skinned and thrown about like sheep without a shepherd." (Matthew 9:35, 36) Jesus felt for the common people. He was keenly aware of their miserable spiritual condition. He knew that they were mistreated and utterly neglected by the very ones who

15, 16. Describe two incidents that reveal how Jesus viewed the people to whom he preached.

should have been shepherding them—the religious leaders. Motivated by deep compassion, Jesus worked hard to reach the people with a message of hope. There was nothing they needed more than the good news of God's Kingdom.

[16] Something similar happened a number of months later, near Passover time in 32 C.E. On this occasion, Jesus and his apostles boarded a boat and sailed across the Sea of Galilee in search of a quiet place to rest. But a crowd of people ran along the shore and arrived on the other side ahead of the boat. How did Jesus react? "On getting out, he saw a great crowd, but he was moved with pity for them, because they were as sheep without a shepherd. And he started to teach them many things." (Mark 6:31-34) Again, Jesus was "moved with pity" because of the poor spiritual condition of the people. Like "sheep without a shepherd," they were starving spiritually and left to fend for themselves. Compassion rather than a mere sense of duty motivated Jesus to preach.

[17] What motivates us as followers of Jesus to share in the ministry? As we saw in Chapter 9 of this book, we have a commission, a responsibility, to preach and to make disciples. (Matthew 28:19, 20; 1 Corinthians 9:16) But our motive for sharing in this work must go beyond a mere sense of duty or obligation. Above all, love for Jehovah moves us to preach the good news of his Kingdom. Our preaching is also motivated by compassion for those who do not share our beliefs. (Mark 12:28-31) How, then, can we cultivate compassion for others?

[18] We need to see people as Jesus saw them—"skinned and thrown about like sheep without a shepherd." Imag-

17, 18. (a) What motivates us to share in the ministry? (b) How can we cultivate compassion for others?

ine finding a lamb that is hopelessly lost. Without a shepherd to lead it to green pastures and water, the poor creature is starving and thirsty. Would not your heart go out to that lamb? Would you not do your best to give it some food and drink? That lamb is like many people who do not yet know the good news. Neglected by false religious shepherds, they are starving and thirsting spiritually and without a real hope for the future. We have what they need: the nourishing spiritual food and refreshing waters of truth found in God's Word. (Isaiah 55:1, 2) When we reflect on the spiritual needs of those around us, our heart goes out to them. If, like Jesus, we feel deeply for people, we will do all we can to share the Kingdom hope with them.

¹⁹ How can we help others to follow Jesus' example? Suppose we want to encourage a Bible student who qualifies to begin sharing in the public preaching work. Or perhaps we want to help an inactive one to have a full share in the ministry again. How can we assist such ones? We need to appeal to their heart. Recall that first Jesus was "moved with pity" for people, and then he taught them. (Mark 6:34) So if we can help them to cultivate compassion, their hearts may well move them to be like Jesus and share the good news with others. We might ask them: "How has accepting the

Preach with compassion

How Can You Follow Jesus?

• In what way did Jesus show compassion in the way he exercised authority, and how can we imitate him?—Matthew 11:28-30.

• Why is it important that we follow Jesus' example in showing mercy, or compassion, to others?—Matthew 9:9-13; 23:23.

• What actions of Jesus demonstrated that he understood the feelings of others, and how can we follow his example? —Luke 7:36-50.

• How does the parable of the neighborly Samaritan show that compassion is a positive quality, and in what way can we apply the point of the story?—Luke 10:29-37.

Kingdom message changed your life for the better? What about people who do not yet know this message—do they not also need the good news? What can you do to help them?" Of course, the strongest motivation for sharing in the ministry is love for God and a desire to serve him.

²⁰ Being a follower of Jesus involves more than just repeating his words and copying his deeds. We need to cultivate the same "mental attitude" that he had. (Philippians 2:5) How thankful we can be, then, that the Bible reveals to us the thoughts and feelings behind Jesus' words and actions! By becoming familiar with "the mind of Christ," we will be better able to cultivate sensitivity and heartfelt compassion and thus treat others the way Jesus treated people in general. (1 Corinthians 2:16) In the next chapter, we will consider the various ways that Jesus showed love for his followers in particular.

_____

20. (a) What is involved in being a follower of Jesus? (b) What will be considered in the next chapter?

CHAPTER 16

"Jesus . . . Loved Them to the End"

AS HE gathers his apostles in an upper room of a house in Jerusalem, Jesus knows that this is his last evening with them. The time is near for him to return to his Father. In a matter of hours, Jesus will be arrested and his faith tested as never before. Yet, not even his impending death can distract him from the needs of the apostles.

² Jesus has prepared the apostles for his departure, but he still has more to say to strengthen them for what lies ahead. So he spends these last precious moments teaching them vital lessons that will help them to remain faithful. His words are among the warmest and most intimate that he has ever shared with them. Why, though, is Jesus more concerned about his apostles than about himself? Why are these final hours with them so dear to him? The answer is, in a word, love. His love for them is profound.

³ Decades later when introducing his inspired account of the events of that evening, the apostle John wrote: "Because he knew before the festival of the passover that his hour had come for him to move out of this world to the Father, Jesus, having loved his own that were in the world, loved them to the end." (John 13:1) Jesus did not wait until that night to demonstrate love to "his own." Throughout his ministry, in ways large and small, he gave proof of his love for his disciples. We do well to examine some of

1, 2. How does Jesus spend his last evening with his apostles, and why are these final moments precious to him?

3. How do we know that Jesus did not wait until his final evening to show love to his followers?

the ways he showed his love, for by imitating him in this regard, we prove ourselves his genuine disciples.

Showing Patience

⁴ Love and patience go together. "Love is long-suffering," observes 1 Corinthians 13:4, and long-suffering involves patiently putting up with others. Did Jesus need patience in dealing with his disciples? Indeed, he did! As we saw in Chapter 3, the apostles were slow to cultivate humility. More than once, they got into arguments about who was the greatest among them. How did Jesus react? Did he get angry and respond with irritation or resentment? No, he patiently reasoned with them, even when "a heated dispute" over this issue arose on his last evening with them! —Luke 22:24-30; Matthew 20:20-28; Mark 9:33-37.

⁵ Later on that final night, when Jesus went to the garden of Gethsemane with the 11 faithful apostles, his patience was tested yet again. Leaving eight of the apostles, Jesus took Peter, James, and John deeper into the garden. "My soul is deeply grieved, even to death," Jesus told them. "Stay here and keep on the watch." He went a short distance away and began praying fervently. After praying at length, he returned to the three apostles. What did he find? In this, his hour of greatest trial, they were fast asleep! Did he berate them for their lack of vigilance? No, he patiently exhorted them. His kind words showed an understanding of the stress they had been under and of their weaknesses.* "The spirit, of course, is eager," he said, "but the flesh is

---

* The apostles' sleepiness was induced by more than physical tiredness. The parallel account at Luke 22:45 says that Jesus "found them slumbering from grief."

4, 5. (a) Why did Jesus need patience in dealing with his disciples? (b) How did Jesus respond when three of his apostles showed a lack of vigilance in the garden of Gethsemane?

weak." Jesus remained patient that evening, even when he came and found them asleep not one but two more times! —Matthew 26:36-46.

⁶ It is encouraging to note that Jesus did not give up on his apostles. His patience eventually bore fruit, for these faithful men learned the importance of being both humble and vigilant. (1 Peter 3:8; 4:7) How can we imitate Jesus in our dealings with others? Elders especially need to exercise patience. Fellow believers may approach an elder with their problems when the elder himself is tired out or distracted by his own concerns. At times, those in need of help may be slow to respond to counsel. Nevertheless, patient elders will instruct "with mildness" and will "treat the flock with tenderness." (2 Timothy 2:24, 25; Acts 20:28, 29) Parents also do well to imitate Jesus in showing patience, for at times children may be slow to respond to counsel or correction. Love and patience will help parents not to give up in their efforts to train their children. The rewards of such patience can be great indeed.—Psalm 127:3.

Caring for Their Needs

⁷ Love is evidenced by unselfish deeds. (1 John 3:17, 18) It "does not look for its own interests." (1 Corinthians 13:5) Love moved Jesus to care for the physical and material needs of his disciples. He often acted in their behalf even before they voiced their needs. When he saw that they were tired, he suggested that they accompany him "privately into a lonely place and rest up a bit." (Mark 6:31) When he sensed that they were hungry, he took the initiative to feed them—along with thousands of others who had come to hear him teach.—Matthew 14:19, 20; 15:35-37.

6. How can we imitate Jesus in our dealings with others?
7. In what ways did Jesus care for the physical and material needs of his disciples?

⁸ Jesus recognized the spiritual needs of his disciples and provided for them. (Matthew 4:4; 5:3) In his teaching, he often gave them special attention. The Sermon on the Mount was delivered especially for the benefit of his disciples. (Matthew 5:1, 2, 13-16) When he taught with illustrations, "privately to his disciples he would explain all things." (Mark 4:34) Jesus appointed a "faithful and discreet slave" to ensure that His followers would be well-fed spiritually after His return to heaven. This slave class, composed of Jesus' spirit-anointed brothers on earth, has been faithfully providing spiritual "food at the proper time" ever since the first century C.E.—Matthew 24:45.

⁹ On the day of his death, Jesus showed in a touching way his concern for the spiritual welfare of his loved ones. Picture the scene. Jesus was on the stake, suffering excruciat-

---

8, 9. (a) What indicates that Jesus recognized the spiritual needs of his disciples and provided for them? (b) When on the stake, how did Jesus show his deep concern for the welfare of his mother?

Caring parents show patience and provide for the needs of their children

ing pain. In order to draw breath, he evidently had to push himself up with his feet. This no doubt caused him severe pain as the weight of his body tore at the nail wounds in his feet and his scourged back rubbed against the stake. Speech, which involves breath control, must have been difficult and painful. Yet, just before he died, Jesus spoke words that showed his deep love for his mother, Mary. Seeing Mary and the apostle John standing nearby, Jesus, in a voice loud enough for bystanders to hear, said to his mother: "Woman, see! Your son!" Then to John, he said: "See! Your mother!" (John 19:26, 27) Jesus knew that the faithful apostle would care not just for Mary's physical and material needs but also for her spiritual welfare.*

[10] Caring parents find it beneficial to reflect on Jesus'

---

* Mary was apparently a widow by then, and her other children were evidently not yet disciples of Jesus.—John 7:5.

---

10. How can parents imitate Jesus as they care for the needs of their children?

example. A father who truly loves his family will provide for them materially. (1 Timothy 5:8) Balanced, loving family heads make time for occasional rest and recreation. More important, Christian parents provide for their children's spiritual needs. How? Such parents arrange for a regular family Bible study, and they endeavor to make these study sessions upbuilding and enjoyable for their children. (Deuteronomy 6:6, 7) By word and example, the parents teach their children that the ministry is an important activity and that preparing for and attending Christian meetings is an essential part of their spiritual routine.—Hebrews 10: 24, 25.

Willing to Forgive

[11] Forgiveness is a facet of love. (Colossians 3:13, 14) Love "does not keep account of the injury," states 1 Corinthians 13:5. On a number of occasions, Jesus taught his followers the importance of forgiveness. He urged them to forgive others "not, Up to seven times, but, Up to seventy-seven times"—that is, an unlimited number of times. (Matthew 18:21, 22) He taught them that a sinner should be forgiven if upon being rebuked, he shows repentance. (Luke 17:3, 4) Jesus, however, was not like the hypocritical Pharisees, who taught by word only; he also taught by example. (Matthew 23:2-4) Let us see how Jesus demonstrated his willingness to forgive even when a trusted friend let him down.

[12] Jesus had a close relationship with the apostle Peter, a warmhearted man who at times was impulsive. Jesus

---

11. What did Jesus teach his followers about forgiveness?
12, 13. (a) In what way did Peter let Jesus down on the night of His arrest? (b) How did Jesus' actions after his resurrection make it clear that he did more than just preach forgiveness?

recognized the good qualities of Peter and extended special privileges to him. Peter, along with James and John, personally witnessed certain miracles that the rest of the 12 did not get to see. (Matthew 17:1, 2; Luke 8:49-55) As we noted earlier, Peter was one of the apostles who accompanied Jesus farther into the garden of Gethsemane on the night of His arrest. Yet, that same night when Jesus was betrayed and taken into custody, Peter and the other apostles abandoned Jesus and fled. Later, Peter proved brave enough to stand outside while Jesus was illegally tried. Still, Peter then became fearful and made a serious mistake—three times he lyingly denied that he even knew Jesus! (Matthew 26:69-75) How did Jesus react? How would you have responded if a close friend let you down in such a way?

[13] Jesus was prepared to forgive Peter. He knew that Peter was crushed by the weight of his sin. After all, the repentant apostle "broke down and gave way to weeping." (Mark 14:72) On the day of His resurrection, Jesus appeared to Peter, likely to comfort and reassure the apostle. (Luke 24:34; 1 Corinthians 15:5) Less than two months later, Jesus dignified Peter by letting him take the lead in giving a witness to the crowds in Jerusalem on the day of Pentecost. (Acts 2:14-40) Let us remember, too, that Jesus did not hold a grudge against the apostles as a group for abandoning him. On the contrary, after his resurrection, he still called them "my brothers." (Matthew 28:10) Is it not clear that Jesus did more than just preach forgiveness?

[14] As disciples of Christ, we need to learn to forgive oth-

---

14. Why do we need to learn to forgive others, and how can we demonstrate a readiness to forgive?

ers. Why? Unlike Jesus, we are imperfect—as are those who may sin against us. From time to time, we all stumble in word and in deed. (Romans 3:23; James 3:2) By forgiving others when there is a basis for mercy, we clear the way for our own sins to be forgiven by God. (Mark 11:25) How, then, can we demonstrate a readiness to forgive those who may sin against us? In many cases, love helps us to overlook the minor sins and shortcomings of others. (1 Peter 4:8) When those who have wronged us are sincerely repentant, as Peter was, surely we want to imitate Jesus' willingness to forgive. Rather than holding a grudge, we wisely choose to let go of resentment. (Ephesians 4:32) By doing so, we contribute to the peace of the congregation as well as to our own peace of mind and heart.—1 Peter 3:11.

Demonstrating His Trust

¹⁵ Love and trust go hand in hand. Love "believes all things."* (1 Corinthians 13:7) Moved by love, Jesus demonstrated a willingness to trust his disciples despite their imperfections. He had confidence in them and believed that at heart they really loved Jehovah and wanted to do His will. Even when they made mistakes, Jesus did not question their motives. For example, when the apostles James and John evidently got their mother to request that they sit beside Jesus in his Kingdom, Jesus did not doubt their loyalty or dismiss them as apostles.—Matthew 20:20-28.

---

* This, of course, does not mean that love is gullible or naive. It means, rather, that love is not unduly critical or suspicious. Love refrains from hastily judging the motives of others or concluding the worst about them.

---

15. Why did Jesus trust his disciples despite their shortcomings?

[16] Demonstrating his trust, Jesus delegated various responsibilities to his disciples. On the two occasions when he miraculously multiplied food and fed the crowds, he delegated to his disciples the responsibility of distributing the food. (Matthew 14:19; 15:36) In preparation for his final Passover, he assigned Peter and John to go to Jerusalem and get things ready. They took care of obtaining the lamb, wine, unleavened bread, bitter greens, and any other necessary items. This was no menial assignment, for celebrating the Passover in the proper manner was a requirement of the Mosaic Law, and Jesus had to live up to that Law. Besides, later that evening Jesus used the wine and the unleavened bread as important symbols when instituting the Memorial of his death.—Matthew 26:17-19; Luke 22:8, 13.

[17] Jesus saw fit to entrust his disciples with even weightier responsibilities. As we noted earlier, he delegated to his anointed followers on earth the important responsibility of dispensing spiritual food. (Luke 12:42-44) Recall, too, that he placed in the hands of his disciples the weighty commission to preach and make disciples. (Matthew 28:18-20) Even now, though invisible and ruling from heaven, Jesus entrusts his congregation on earth to the care of spiritually qualified "gifts in men."—Ephesians 4:8, 11, 12.

[18] How can we follow Jesus' example in our dealings with others? Our showing trust and confidence in fellow believers is an expression of our love. Let us remember that love is positive, not negative. When others dis-

---

16, 17. What responsibilities did Jesus delegate to his disciples?
18-20. (a) How can we show trust and confidence in fellow believers? (b) How can we imitate Jesus' willingness to delegate? (c) What will be discussed in the next chapter?

How Can You Follow Jesus?

• Why is it important for us to heed Jesus' counsel about forgiveness?—Matthew 6:14, 15.

• How can we apply the point of Jesus' illustration about the need for us to be forgiving?—Matthew 18:23-35.

• How did Jesus show consideration for his disciples, and how can we imitate him?—Matthew 20:17-19; John 16:12.

• How did Jesus let Peter know that He had confidence in him, and how can we express confidence in others?—Luke 22: 31, 32.

appoint us, which is bound to happen from time to time, love will keep us from quickly assuming that their motives are bad. (Matthew 7:1, 2) If we keep a positive view of our fellow believers, we will treat them in ways that build up rather than tear down.—1 Thessalonians 5:11.

¹⁹ Can we imitate Jesus' willingness to delegate? It is beneficial for those who have positions of responsibility in the congregation to delegate appropriate and meaningful tasks to others, trusting them to do their best. Experienced elders can thereby provide necessary and valuable training for qualified younger men who are "reaching out" to help in the congregation. (1 Timothy 3:1; 2 Timothy 2:2) This training is vital. As Jehovah continues to speed up Kingdom growth, qualified men will need to be trained to care for the increase.—Isaiah 60:22.

²⁰ Jesus provided us with a marvelous example in showing love to others. Of all the ways that we can follow him, imitating his love is the most important. In the next chapter, we will discuss the greatest expression of his love for us—his willingness to give his life.

CHAPTER 17

"No One Has Love Greater Than This"

"LOOK! The man!" With those words, the Roman Governor Pontius Pilate presents Jesus Christ to the angry mob gathered outside the governor's palace at dawn on Passover of 33 C.E. (John 19:5) Just a few days earlier, Jesus was hailed by the crowds when he made his triumphal entry into Jerusalem as the divinely appointed King. On this night, however, the hostile crowd has a very different view of him.

² Jesus is decked with a purple robe like that worn by royalty, and he has a crown upon his head. But the robe, covering the ribbons of bleeding flesh on his scourged back, and the crown, braided of thorns and pressed into his now-bloodied scalp, are in mockery of his royal status. The people, incited by the chief priests, reject the battered man standing before them. The priests shout: "Impale him! Impale him!" With murder in their hearts, the people cry out: "He ought to die."—John 19:1-7.

³ With dignity and courage, Jesus endures the humiliation and suffering uncomplainingly.* He is fully prepared

---

* Twice that day Jesus was spit upon, first by the religious leaders and then by the Roman soldiers. (Matthew 26:59-68; 27:27-30) Even this contemptuous treatment, he took without complaining, fulfilling the prophetic words: "My face I did not conceal from humiliating things and spit."—Isaiah 50:6.

1-4. (a) What happens when Pilate presents Jesus to the angry mob gathered outside the governor's palace? (b) How does Jesus respond to the humiliation and suffering, and what important questions are raised?

to die. Later that Passover Day, he willingly submits to a painful death on a torture stake.—John 19:17, 18, 30.

[4] By surrendering his life, Jesus proved himself a real friend to his followers. "No one has love greater than this," he said, "that someone should surrender his soul in behalf of his friends." (John 15:13) That raises some important questions. Was it really necessary for Jesus to go through all that suffering and then to die? Why was he willing to do so? As "his friends" and followers, how can we imitate his example?

Why Was It Necessary for Jesus to Suffer and Die?

[5] As the promised Messiah, Jesus knew what to expect. He was aware of the many prophecies in the Hebrew Scriptures that foretold in detail the Messiah's suffering and death. (Isaiah 53:3-7, 12; Daniel 9:26) More than once, he prepared his disciples for the trials that awaited him. (Mark 8:31; 9:31) On the way to Jerusalem for his final Passover, he specifically told his apostles: "The Son of man will be delivered to the chief priests and the scribes, and they will condemn him to death and will deliver him to men of the nations, and they will make fun of him and will spit upon him and scourge him and kill him." (Mark 10:33, 34) These were no empty words. As we have seen, Jesus was indeed made fun of, spit upon, scourged, and killed.

[6] Why, though, was it necessary for Jesus to suffer and die? For several profoundly significant reasons. First, by keeping loyal, Jesus would prove his integrity and uphold Jehovah's sovereignty. Recall that Satan falsely claimed

---

5. How did Jesus know the specific trials that awaited him?
6. Why was it necessary for Jesus to suffer and die?

that humans serve God only out of selfish interest. (Job 2:
1-5) By remaining faithful "as far as death . . . on a torture stake," Jesus gave the most conclusive answer possible to Satan's baseless charge. (Philippians 2:8; Proverbs
27:11) Second, the Messiah's suffering and death would
provide atonement for the sins of others. (Isaiah 53:5, 10;
Daniel 9:24) Jesus gave "his soul a ransom in exchange
for many," opening the way for us to have an approved
relationship with God. (Matthew 20:28) Third, by enduring all manner of hardships and suffering, Jesus was "tested in all respects like ourselves." He is thus a compassion-
ate High Priest, one who is able to "sympathize with our
weaknesses."—Hebrews 2:17, 18; 4:15.

Why Was Jesus Willing to Give His Life?

⁷ To put into perspective what Jesus was willing to do,
think about this: What man would leave his family and
home and move to a foreign land if he knew that most
of its inhabitants would reject him, that he would be subjected to humiliation and suffering, and that he would
finally be murdered? Consider now what Jesus did. Before
coming to earth, he had a favored position in the heavens alongside his Father. Yet, Jesus willingly left his heavenly home and came to earth as a human. He made this
move, knowing that he would be rejected by the majori-
ty and that he would be subjected to cruel humiliation,
intense suffering, and a painful death. (Philippians 2:5-7)
What motivated Jesus to make such a sacrifice?

⁸ Above all, Jesus was impelled by deep love for his
Father. Jesus' endurance was evidence of his love for
Jehovah. That love caused Jesus to be concerned about his

7. How much did Jesus give up when he came to earth?
8, 9. What motivated Jesus to surrender his life?

Father's name and reputation. (Matthew 6:9; John 17:1-6, 26) More than anything, Jesus wanted to see his Father's name cleared of the reproach that had been heaped upon it. Jesus thus counted it the highest honor and privilege to suffer for righteousness' sake, for he knew that his integrity would play a part in sanctifying his Father's good and beautiful name.—1 Chronicles 29:13.

⁹ Jesus had another motive for laying down his life—love for humankind. This is a love that goes back to the very beginning of human history. Long before Jesus came to earth, the Bible reveals that he felt this way: "The things I was fond of were with the sons of men." (Proverbs 8:30, 31) His love was clearly evident when he was on earth. As we saw in the preceding three chapters of this book, in many ways Jesus showed his love for humans in general and for his followers in particular. But on Nisan 14, 33 C.E., he willingly gave his soul in our behalf. (John 10: 11) Truly, there was no greater way for him to demonstrate his love for us. Are we to imitate him in this regard? Yes. In fact, we are commanded to do so.

"Love One Another . . . as I Have Loved You"

¹⁰ The night before he died, Jesus told his closest disciples: "I am giving you a new commandment, that you love one another; just as I have loved you, that you also love one another. By this all will know that you are my disciples, if you have love among yourselves." (John 13: 34, 35) "Love one another"—why is that "a new commandment"? The Mosaic Law had already commanded: "You must love your fellow [or, neighbor] as yourself." (Leviticus 19:18) But the new commandment calls for a

---

10, 11. What is the new commandment that Jesus gave his followers, what does it involve, and why is it important that we obey it?

greater love, a love that would move us to give our own life in behalf of others. Jesus himself made this clear when he said: "This is my commandment, that you love one another just as I have loved you. No one has love greater than this, that someone should surrender his soul in behalf of his friends." (John 15:12, 13) The new commandment, in effect, says: "Love others, not *as* yourself, but *more than* yourself." By his life and death, Jesus certainly exemplified such love.

[11] Why is it important that we obey the new commandment? Recall that Jesus said: "By this [self-sacrificing love] all will know that you are my disciples." Yes, self-sacrificing love identifies us as true Christians. We might compare this love to an identification badge. Delegates attending the annual conventions of Jehovah's Witnesses wear badge cards. The card identifies the wearer, showing his name and congregation. Self-sacrificing love for one another is the "badge" that identifies genuine Christians. In other words, the love we show one another should be so noticeable that it would serve as a sign, or badge, telling observers that we are indeed true followers of Christ. Each of us does well to ask himself, 'Is the "badge" of self-sacrificing love evident in my life?'

Self-Sacrificing Love—What Does It Involve?

[12] As followers of Jesus, we need to love one another as he loved us. This means being willing to make sacrifices for fellow believers. How far must we be willing to go? The Bible tells us: "By this we have come to know love, because that one surrendered his soul for us; and we are under obligation to surrender our souls for our brothers."

12, 13. (a) How far must we be willing to go to demonstrate our love for one another? (b) What does it mean to be self-sacrificing?

(1 John 3:16) Like Jesus, we must be willing to die for one another if necessary. In times of persecution, we would rather sacrifice our own life than betray our spiritual brothers and thus endanger their lives. In lands divided by racial or ethnic strife, we would risk our own lives to protect our brothers, regardless of their racial or ethnic background. When nations go to war, we would sooner face imprisonment or even death than take up weapons against fellow believers—or anyone else for that matter. —John 17:14, 16; 1 John 3:10-12.

13 Being willing to lay down our life for our brothers is not the only way to show self-sacrificing love. After all, few of us are ever called upon to make such a great sacrifice. However, if we love our brothers enough to die for them, should we not be willing to make smaller sacrifices, going out of our way to help them now? To be self-sacrificing means to give up our own advantage or comfort for the benefit of others. We put their needs and welfare ahead of our own even if it is not convenient. (1 Corinthians 10:24) In what practical ways can we show self-sacrificing love?

In the Congregation and in the Family

14 Congregation elders make many sacrifices to "shepherd the flock." (1 Peter 5:2, 3) In addition to looking after their own families, they may need to take time during evenings or on weekends to care for congregation matters, including preparing meeting parts, making shepherding calls, and handling judicial cases. Many elders make additional sacrifices, working hard at assemblies and conventions and serving as members of Hospital Liaison Committees, Patient Visitation Groups, and Regional Building

14. (a) Elders are called upon to make what sacrifices? (b) How do you feel about the hardworking elders in your congregation?

Committees. Elders, never forget that by serving with a willing spirit—spending your time, energy, and resources shepherding the flock—you are showing self-sacrificing love. (2 Corinthians 12:15) Your unselfish efforts are appreciated not only by Jehovah but also by the congregation you shepherd.—Philippians 2:29; Hebrews 6:10.

¹⁵ What, though, about the wives of elders—do not these supportive women also make sacrifices so that their husbands can take care of the flock? Surely it is a sacrifice for a wife when her husband needs to devote to congregation matters time that he might otherwise spend with his family. Think, too, of the wives of traveling overseers and the sacrifices they make to accompany their husbands from congregation to congregation and from circuit to circuit. They forgo having a home of their own and perhaps have to sleep in a different bed each week. Wives who willingly put the interests of the congregation ahead of their own are to be commended for their generous expressions of self-sacrificing love.—Philippians 2:3, 4.

¹⁶ How can we show self-sacrificing love in the family? Parents, you make many sacrifices to provide for your children and to bring them up "in the discipline and mental-regulating of Jehovah." (Ephesians 6:4) You may have to work long hours at exhausting jobs just to put food on the table and to be sure that your children have adequate clothing and shelter. You would rather do with less for yourself than see your children deprived of life's necessities. You also expend much effort to study with your children, take them to Christian meetings, and work

---

15. (a) What are some of the sacrifices made by the wives of elders? (b) How do you feel about the supportive wives who share their husbands with your congregation?
16. Christian parents make what sacrifices for their children?

along with them in the field ministry. (Deuteronomy 6: 6, 7) Your self-sacrificing love pleases the Originator of family life and may mean everlasting life for your children.—Proverbs 22:6; Ephesians 3:14, 15.

[17] Husbands, how can you imitate Jesus in showing self-sacrificing love? The Bible answers: "Husbands, continue loving your wives, just as the Christ also loved the congregation and delivered up himself for it." (Ephesians 5: 25) As we have seen, Jesus loved his followers so much that he died for them. A Christian husband imitates the unselfish attitude of Jesus, who "did not please himself." (Romans 15:3) Such a husband willingly puts his wife's needs and interests before his own. He does not rigidly insist on having his own way, but he shows a willingness to yield when there is no Scriptural issue involved. The husband who shows self-sacrificing love gains Jehovah's approval and wins the love and respect of his wife and children.

What Will You Do?

[18] Obeying the new commandment to love one another is not an easy course to follow, but we have a powerful motivation for doing so. Paul wrote: "The love the Christ has compels us, because this is what we have judged, that one man died for all . . . , and he died for all that those who live might live no longer for themselves, but for him who died for them and was raised up." (2 Corinthians 5: 14, 15) Since Jesus died for us, should we not feel compelled to live for him? We can do that by following his example of self-sacrificing love.

---

17. How can Christian husbands imitate the unselfish attitude of Jesus?
18. What motivates us to follow the new commandment to love one another?

How Can You Follow Jesus?

• What unselfish course did Jesus outline for his followers to take?—Matthew 16:24-26.

• Why is a self-sacrificing course worthwhile?—Mark 10: 23-30.

• How did Jesus prove himself to be the Fine Shepherd, and what can Christian elders learn from his example?—John 10:11-15.

• In what practical ways can we imitate Jesus in showing self-sacrificing love?—1 John 3:17, 18.

¹⁹ Jesus was not exaggerating when he said: "No one has love greater than this, that someone should surrender his soul in behalf of his friends." (John 15:13) His willingness to surrender his soul in our behalf was the greatest expression of *his* love for us. Yet, someone else has shown us even greater love. Jesus explained: "God loved the world so much that he gave his only-begotten Son, in order that everyone exercising faith in him might not be destroyed but have everlasting life." (John 3:16) God loves us so much that he gave his Son as a ransom, making it possible for us to be delivered from sin and death. (Ephesians 1:7) The ransom is a precious gift from Jehovah, but he does not force us to accept it.

²⁰ It is up to us to accept Jehovah's gift. How? By "exercising faith" in his Son. Faith, however, is not just words. It is proved by actions, by the way we live. (James 2:26) We prove our faith in Jesus Christ by following him day after day. Doing so will bring rich blessings now and in the future, as the final chapter of this book will explain.

19, 20. What precious gift has Jehovah given us, and how can we show that we accept it?

CHAPTER 18

"Continue Following Me"

ELEVEN men stand together on a mountain. With great love and admiration, they look upon a 12th figure. He is human in form, but in fact he is the resurrected Jesus, once again the mightiest of Jehovah's spirit sons. Jesus has gathered his apostles to meet with him here on the Mount of Olives for one last time.

2 This mount, part of a chain of limestone hills across the Kidron Valley from Jerusalem, surely brings a wealth of memories to Jesus' mind. On these slopes lies the town of Bethany, where Jesus resurrected Lazarus. Just weeks ago, Jesus set out on his triumphal ride into Jerusalem from nearby Bethphage. The Mount of Olives is also the probable site of the garden of Gethsemane, where Jesus spent the agonizing hours before his arrest. Now on this same hill, Jesus prepares to leave his closest friends and followers behind. He utters kind parting words. Then he begins to rise from the earth! The apostles stand there rooted to the spot, gazing after their beloved Master as he ascends into the sky. Finally, a cloud obscures him from their view, and they see him no more.—Acts 1:6-12.

3 Does that scene strike you as a bittersweet ending, a forlorn farewell? It is not. In fact, as two angels now remind the apostles, Jesus' story is far from over. (Acts 1: 10, 11) In many ways, his departure toward heaven is just a beginning. God's Word does not leave us in the dark

---

1-3. (a) In what manner did Jesus leave his apostles, and why was that not a forlorn farewell? (b) Why do we need to learn about the life Jesus has led since returning to heaven?

about what next happened to Jesus. Learning about the life Jesus has led since leaving the earth is important. Why? Remember the words Jesus spoke to Peter: "Continue following me." (John 21:19, 22) We all need to obey that command, not merely as a momentary choice but as a way of life. In order to do so, we need to understand what our Master is doing now and the assignments he has received in heaven.

The Life Jesus Has Led Since Leaving the Earth

[4] Regarding Jesus' arrival in heaven, his welcome, and his joyous reunion with his Father, the Scriptures are silent. However, the Bible did reveal in advance what would happen in heaven soon after Jesus' return there. You see, for over 15 centuries, the Jewish people had regularly witnessed a holy ceremony. One day each year, the high priest entered the Most Holy of the temple to sprinkle the blood of the Atonement Day sacrifices before the ark of the covenant. On that day, the high priest pictured the Messiah. Jesus fulfilled the prophetic meaning of that ceremony once for all time after he returned to heaven. He came into Jehovah's majestic presence in heaven —the holiest place in the universe—and presented to his Father the value of his ransom sacrifice. (Hebrews 9:11, 12, 24) Did Jehovah accept it?

[5] We find the answer by considering what happened a few days after Jesus' ascension. A small band of about 120 Christians were meeting in Jerusalem in an upstairs room when suddenly a noise like a stiff rushing breeze filled the place. Tongues as if of fire appeared above their

---

4. How did the Bible reveal in advance what would happen in heaven after Jesus' return there?
5, 6. (a) What evidence showed that Jehovah had accepted Christ's ransom sacrifice? (b) Who benefit from the ransom, and how?

heads, they were filled with holy spirit, and they began speaking in various tongues. (Acts 2:1-4) This event signified the birth of a new nation, spiritual Israel, which was God's new "chosen race" and "royal priesthood" for carrying out the divine will on earth. (1 Peter 2:9) Clearly, Jehovah God had accepted and approved Christ's ransom sacrifice. This outpouring of holy spirit was among the first blessings made possible by the ransom.

⁶ Ever since then, Christ's ransom has benefited his followers the world over. Whether we are among the anointed "little flock," who will rule with Christ in heaven, or are among the "other sheep," who will live under his rule on earth, we benefit from his sacrifice. (Luke 12: 32; John 10:16) It is the basis for our hope and for forgiveness of our sins. As long as we continue "exercising faith" in that ransom, following Jesus day by day, we can enjoy a clean conscience and a bright hope for the future. —John 3:16.

⁷ What has Jesus been doing in heaven since his return there? He has tremendous authority. (Matthew 28:18) Indeed, Jehovah appointed him to rule over the Christian congregation, an assignment that he has carried out in a loving and just way. (Colossians 1:13) As foretold, Jesus has provided responsible men to care for the needs of his flock. (Ephesians 4:8) For example, he chose Paul to be "an apostle to the nations," sending him to spread the good news far and wide. (Romans 11:13; 1 Timothy 2:7) Near the end of the first century, Jesus directed messages of commendation, counsel, and correction to seven congregations in the Roman province of Asia. (Revelation, chapters 2-3) Do you recognize Jesus as Head of

7. Jesus was granted what authority after returning to heaven, and how may you support him?

the Christian congregation? (Ephesians 5:23) In order to continue following him, you will want to promote an obedient, cooperative spirit in your local congregation.

[8] Jesus was granted still more authority in 1914. In that year he was appointed as King of Jehovah's Messianic Kingdom. When Jesus' rule began, "war broke out in heaven." The result? Satan and his demons were hurled to the earth, triggering an era of woe. The rampant wars, crime, terror, disease, earthquakes, and famines that have afflicted modern man remind us that Jesus is ruling in heaven right now. Satan is still "the ruler of this world" for "a short period of time." (Revelation 12:7-12; John 12:31; Matthew 24:3-7; Luke 21:11) However, Jesus is giving people worldwide the opportunity to accept His rulership.

[9] It is vital that we take our stand on the side of the Messianic King. In all our daily decisions, we must seek his approval, not that of this corrupt world. As this "King of kings and Lord of lords" surveys mankind, his righteous heart blazes with anger and overflows with joy. (Revelation 19:16) Why?

The Anger and the Joy of the Messianic King

[10] Like his Father, our Master is by nature happy. (1 Timothy 1:11) As a man, Jesus was neither critical nor hard to please. Yet, there is much happening on the earth today that must fill him with righteous anger. He is certainly angry at all those religious organizations that falsely claim to represent him. He foretold as much: "Not

---

8, 9. What authority was Jesus granted in 1914, and what should that mean for us in the decisions we make?

10. What is Jesus' natural disposition, yet what fills our Master with righteous anger?

everyone saying to me, 'Lord, Lord,' will enter into the kingdom of the heavens, but the one doing the will of my Father who is in the heavens will. Many will say to me in that day, 'Lord, Lord, did we not . . . perform many powerful works in your name?' And yet then I will confess to them: I never knew you! Get away from me, you workers of lawlessness."—Matthew 7:21-23.

[11] Many today who call themselves Christians might find those words puzzling. Why would Jesus direct such strong words to people who have been performing "many powerful works" in his name? The churches of Christendom have sponsored charities, aided the poor, built hospitals and schools, and performed many other works. To see why they have earned Jesus' anger, consider an illustration.

[12] A father and mother need to go on a trip. They cannot take their children along, so they hire a babysitter. Their instructions to her are simple: "Take care of our children. Feed them, make sure they are clean, and keep them from harm." When the parents return, though, they are shocked to see that their children are famished. They are dirty, sickly, and miserable. They are crying for the babysitter's attention, but their cries go unheeded. Why? She is up on a ladder, washing the windows. Furious, the parents demand an explanation. The sitter replies: "Look at all that I did! Aren't the windows clean? I made repairs to the house too, all for you!" Would the parents feel better? Hardly! They never asked her to do those jobs; they just wanted their children cared for. Her refusal to heed their instructions would infuriate them.

11-13. Why might some be puzzled by the strong words Jesus directed toward those performing "many powerful works" in his name, yet why is he angry? Illustrate.

¹³ Christendom has acted like that babysitter. Jesus left instructions with his representatives to feed people spiritually by teaching them the truth of God's Word and helping them to be spiritually clean. (John 21:15-17) Yet, Christendom has dismally failed to obey his direction. She has left people spiritually starved, confused by falsehoods and ignorant of basic Bible truths. (Isaiah 65:13; Amos 8:11) Even her attempts to better this world can hardly excuse her willful disobedience. After all, this world system is like a house that is slated for demolition! God's Word makes it clear that Satan's world system is soon to be destroyed.—1 John 2:15-17.

¹⁴ On the other hand, Jesus must be very happy to look down from heaven and see that millions of people are fulfilling the disciple-making commission that he gave his followers before leaving the earth. (Matthew 28:19, 20) What a privilege it is to contribute to the joy of the Messianic King! Let us be determined never to give up in assisting "the faithful and discreet slave." (Matthew 24:45) Unlike Christendom's clergy, this class of anointed Christians has obediently spearheaded the preaching work and has faithfully fed Christ's sheep.

¹⁵ We can be sure that the King is angry when he sees the lovelessness that prevails on the earth today. We might recall how the Pharisees criticized Jesus for performing cures on the Sabbath. They were so hardhearted, so set in their ways, that they could not see past their own narrow interpretation of the Mosaic Law and the oral law. Jesus' miracles did good beyond measure!

---

14. What work is making Jesus happy today, and why?

15, 16. (a) How does Jesus feel about the lovelessness so prevalent today, and how do we know that? (b) How has Christendom earned Jesus' anger?

But the joy, the relief, the strengthening of faith that such miracles brought about meant nothing to those men. How did Jesus feel about them? He once looked "around upon them with indignation, being thoroughly grieved at the insensibility of their hearts."—Mark 3:5.

[16] Today, Jesus sees far more to make him feel "thoroughly grieved." The leaders of Christendom are blinded by their devotion to traditions and doctrines that are at odds with the Scriptures. Further, they are enraged by the preaching of the good news of God's Kingdom. In many parts of the world, the clergy have fomented vicious persecution against those Christians who sincerely try to preach the message that Jesus preached. (John 16:2; Revelation 18:4, 24) At the same time, such clergymen often exhort their own followers to go to war and take the lives of others—as if doing so would please Jesus Christ!

[17] In contrast, Jesus' genuine followers endeavor to show love to their fellow man. They share the good news with "all sorts of men," just as Jesus did, despite opposition. (1 Timothy 2:4) And the love they show to one another is outstanding; it is their chief identifying mark. (John 13:34, 35) As they treat their fellow Christians with love, respect, and dignity, they are truly following Jesus —and making the heart of the Messianic King rejoice!

[18] Let us also keep in mind that our Master is distressed when his followers fail to endure, letting their love for Jehovah cool off and giving up as His servants. (Revelation 2:4, 5) However, Jesus is pleased with those who endure to the end. (Matthew 24:13) By all means, then, let us keep ever in mind Christ's command: *"Continue* follow-

---

17. How do Jesus' genuine followers make his heart rejoice?
18. What distresses our Master, yet how may we please him?

ing me." (John 21:19) Let us consider some of the blessings that the Messianic King will bestow on those who endure to the end.

Blessings Flow to Faithful Servants of the King

¹⁹ Following Jesus is the way to a truly blessed life right now. If we accept Christ as our Master, following his direction and using his example as our guide, we will find treasures that people the world over seek in vain. We will be blessed with work that fills our life with purpose and meaning, a family of fellow believers united in a genuine bond of love, a clean conscience, and peace of mind. In short, we will find a life that is rich and satisfying. And we will find still more.

²⁰ In Jesus, Jehovah has provided an "Eternal Father" for those who hope to live forever on earth. Jesus is a replacement for the human father, Adam, who failed all his offspring so miserably. (Isaiah 9:6, 7) By accepting Jesus as our "Eternal Father," exercising faith in him, we have a sure hope of everlasting life. Further, we thereby get ever closer to Jehovah God. As we have learned, striving to follow Jesus' example day by day is the best possible way to obey this divine command: "Become imitators of God, as beloved children."—Ephesians 5:1.

²¹ As we imitate Jesus and his Father, Jehovah, we have a wonderful privilege. We reflect a brilliant light. In a world shrouded in darkness, where billions are misled by Satan and imitate his traits, we who follow Christ spread abroad reflections of the brightest light—the light of Scriptural truths, the light of fine Christian qualities,

---

19, 20. (a) Following Jesus leads to what blessings right now? (b) How can following Christ help us to fill our need for a father?
21. How do followers of Christ reflect light in a dark world?

the light of genuine joy, true peace, real love. At the same time, we draw closer to Jehovah, and that is the ultimate goal, the highest possible aim, of any intelligent creature.

²² Think, too, of what Jehovah wants to do for you in the future by means of his Messianic King. Soon that King will wage righteous warfare against Satan's wicked system of things. Jesus' victory is sure! (Revelation 19:11-15) Afterward, Christ will begin his Thousand Year Reign over the earth. His heavenly government will dispense

22, 23. (a) What future blessings will come to those who loyally continue to follow Jesus? (b) What should be our determination?

How Can You Follow Jesus?

• What will help you to bring your thinking into harmony with that of Christ?—1 Corinthians 2:13-16.

• In what ways do you intend to follow Jesus more closely? —1 Peter 2:21.

• How will you avoid the danger of cooling off in your love for Jesus?—Revelation 3:14-18.

• How can you show that you really want Christ to rule over the earth in the near future?—Revelation 22:17, 20.

---

the benefits of the ransom to every faithful human, raising such ones to perfection. Imagine yourself vibrant in health, ever young and strong, happily working with a united human family to turn this earth into a paradise! At the end of that Millennium, Jesus will hand the rulership back to his Father. (1 Corinthians 15:24) If you continue loyally following Christ, you will be granted a blessing so wonderful that it is hard even to imagine—"the glorious freedom of the children of God"! (Romans 8:21) Yes, we will have all the blessings that Adam and Eve had and lost. Earthly sons and daughters of Jehovah, we will be forever free of the stain of Adam's sin. Truly, "death will be no more."—Revelation 21:4.

23 Recall that wealthy young ruler we discussed in Chapter 1. He turned down Jesus' invitation: "Come be my follower." (Mark 10:17-22) Never make that mistake! May you take hold of Jesus' invitation with joy and enthusiasm. May you be determined to endure, to continue following the Fine Shepherd day by day, year by year, and live to see him bring all of Jehovah's purposes to glorious fulfillment at last!

Would you welcome more information?

Write Jehovah's Witnesses at the appropriate address below.

ALBANIA: Kutia postare 118, Tiranë. **ANGOLA:** Caixa Postal 6877, Luanda Sul. **ANTIGUA:** Box 119, St. Johns. **ARGENTINA:** Casilla de Correo 83 (Suc. 27B), 1427 Buenos Aires. **AUSTRALIA:** Box 280, Ingleburn, NSW 1890. **AUSTRIA:** Postfach 67, A-1134 Vienna. **BAHAMAS:** Box N-1247, Nassau, N.P. **BARBADOS, W.I.:** Crusher Site Road, Prospect, St. James BB 24012. **BELGIUM:** rue d'Argile-Potaardestraat 60, B-1950 Kraainem. **BENIN, REP. OF:** 06 B.P. 1131, Akpakpa pk3, Cotonou. **BOLIVIA:** Casilla 6397, Santa Cruz. **BRAZIL:** Caixa Postal 92, 18270-970 Tatuí, SP. **BRITAIN:** The Ridgeway, London NW7 1RN. **CAMEROON:** B.P. 889, Douala. **CANADA:** Box 4100, Halton Hills (Georgetown), Ontario L7G 4Y4. **CENTRAL AFRICAN REPUBLIC:** B.P. 662, Bangui. **CHILE:** Casilla 267, Puente Alto. **COLOMBIA:** Apartado Postal 85058, Bogotá 8, D.C. **CONGO, DEMOCRATIC REPUBLIC OF:** B.P. 634, Limete, Kinshasa. **COSTA RICA:** Apartado 187-3006, Barreal, Heredia. **CÔTE D'IVOIRE (IVORY COAST), WEST AFRICA:** 06 B P 393, Abidjan 06. **CROATIA:** p.p. 58, HR-10090 Zagreb-Susedgrad. **CURAÇAO, NETHERLANDS ANTILLES:** P.O. Box 4708, Willemstad. **CYPRUS:** P.O. Box 11033, CY-2550 Dali. **CZECH REPUBLIC:** P.O. Box 90, 198 21 Prague 9. **DENMARK:** Stenhusvej 28, DK-4300 Holbæk. **DOMINICAN REPUBLIC:** Apartado 1742, Santo Domingo. **ECUADOR:** Casilla 09-01-1334, Guayaquil. **EL SALVADOR:** Apartado Postal 401, San Salvador. **ESTONIA:** Postbox 1075, 10302 Tallinn. **ETHIOPIA:** P.O. Box 5522, Addis Ababa. **FIJI:** Box 23, Suva. **FINLAND:** Postbox 68, FI-01301 Vantaa. **FRANCE:** B.P. 625, F-27406 Louviers cedex. **GERMANY:** Niederselters, Am Steinfels, D-65618 Selters. **GHANA:** P. O. Box GP 760, Accra. **GREECE:** 77 Kifisias Ave., GR-151 24, Marousi, Athens. **GUADELOUPE:** Monmain, 97180 Sainte Anne. **GUAM 96913:** 143 Jehovah St., Barrigada. **GUATEMALA:** Apartado postal 711, 01901 Guatemala. **GUYANA:** 352-360 Tyrell St., Republic Park Phase 2 EBD. **GUYANE FRANÇAISE (FRENCH GUIANA):** 328 CD2, Route du Tigre, 97300 Cayenne. **HAITI:** Post Box 185, Port-au-Prince. **HAWAII 96819:** 2055 Kam IV Rd., Honolulu. **HONDURAS:** Apartado 147, Tegucigalpa. **HONG KONG:** 4 Kent Road, Kowloon Tong. **HUNGARY:** H-1631 Budapest, Pf. 20. **ICELAND:** Sogavegur 71, IS-108, Reykjavík. **INDIA:** Post Box 6440, Yelahanka, Bangalore 560 064, KAR. **INDONESIA:** P.O. Box 2105, Jakarta 10001. **IRELAND:** Newcastle, Greystones, Co. Wicklow. **ISRAEL:** P.O. Box 29345, Tel Aviv 61293. **ITALY:** Via della Bufalotta 1281, I-00138 Rome RM. **JAMAICA:** P. O. Box 103, Old Harbour, St. Catherine. **JAPAN:** 4-7-1 Nakashinden, Ebina City, Kanagawa Pref., 243-0496. **KENYA:** P. O. Box 47788, GPO Nairobi 00100. **KOREA, REPUBLIC OF:** Box 33 Pyungtaek P. O., Kyunggido, 450-600. **KYRGYZSTAN:** Post Box 80, Bishkek 720080. **LIBERIA:** P. O. Box 10-0380, 1000 Monrovia 10. **LUXEMBOURG:** B. P. 2186, L-1021 Luxembourg, G. D. **MADAGASCAR:** B.P. 116, 105 Ivato. **MALAWI:** Box 30749, Lilongwe 3. **MALAYSIA:** Peti Surat No. 580, 75760 Melaka. **MARTINIQUE:** 20, rue de la Cour Campêche, 97200 Fort de France. **MAURITIUS:** Rue Baissac, Petit Verger, Pointe aux Sables. **MEXICO:** Apartado Postal 896, 06002 Mexico, D. F. **MOZAMBIQUE:** Caixa Postal 2600, Maputo. **MYANMAR:** P.O. Box 62, Yangon. **NETHERLANDS:** Noordbargerstraat 77, NL-7812 AA Emmen. **NEW CALEDONIA:** BP 1741, 98874 Mont Dore. **NEW ZEALAND:** PO Box 75142, Manurewa, Manukau 2243. **NICARAGUA:** Apartado 3587, Managua. **NIGERIA:** P.M.B. 1090, Benin City 300001, Edo State. **NORWAY:** Gaupeveien 24, N-1914 Ytre Enebakk. **PANAMA:** Apartado 0819-07567, Panama. **PAPUA NEW GUINEA:** P. O. Box 636, Boroko, NCD 111. **PARAGUAY:** Casilla de Correo 482, 1209 Asunción. **PERU:** Apartado 18-1055, Lima 18. **PHILIPPINES, REPUBLIC OF:** P. O. Box 2044, 1060 Manila. **POLAND:** ul. Warszawska 14, PL-05-830 Nadarzyn. **PORTUGAL:** Apartado 91, P-2766-955 Estoril. **PUERTO RICO 00970:** P.O. Box 3980, Guaynabo. **ROMANIA:** Căsuţa Poştală nr. 132, Oficiul Poştal nr. 39, Bucureşti. **RUSSIA:** P.O. Box 182. 190000 St. Petersburg. **RWANDA:** B.P. 529, Kigali. **SLOVAKIA:** P. O. Box 2, 830 04 Bratislava 34. **SLOVENIA:** Groharjeva ulica 22, p.p. 22, SI-1241 Kamnik. **SOLOMON ISLANDS:** P.O. Box 166, Honiara. **SOUTH AFRICA:** Private Bag X2067, Krugersdorp, 1740. **SPAIN:** Apartado 132, 28850 Torrejón de Ardoz (Madrid). **SRI LANKA, REP. OF:** 711 Station Road, Wattala 11300. **SURINAME:** P.O. Box 2914, Paramaribo. **SWEDEN:** Box 5, SE-732 21 Arboga. **SWITZERLAND:** PO Box 225, 3602 Thun. **TAHITI:** B.P. 7715, 98719 Taravao. **TAIWAN 32746:** 3-12 Shetze Village, Hsinwu. **TANZANIA:** Box 7992, Dar es Salaam. **THAILAND:** 69/1 Soi Phasuk, Sukhumwit Rd., Soi 2, Bangkok 10110. **TOGO, WEST AFRICA:** B.P. 2983, Lomé. **TRINIDAD AND TOBAGO, REP. OF:** Lower Rapsey Street & Laxmi Lane, Curepe. **UKRAINE:** P.O. Box 246, 79000 Lviv. **UNITED STATES OF AMERICA:** 25 Columbia Heights, Brooklyn, NY 11201-2483. **URUGUAY:** Casilla 17030, 12500 Montevideo. **VENEZUELA:** Apartado 20.364, Caracas, DC 1020A. **ZAMBIA:** Box 33459, Lusaka 10101. **ZIMBABWE:** Private Bag WG-5001, Westgate.

www.watchtower.org